Prais,
Charlotte R
Faulconbridge

"This book will captivate every reader, and is a must read for neurodivergent people, parents, carers, and professionals. Charlotte retells key parts of her life in such a candid, heart-warming, and moving way, that it will have you laughing one moment and crying the next. This book provides such a marvellous insight and leaves you truly in awe of Charlotte and all autistic people."

Kylie Holdback, Specialist Paediatric Occupational Therapist

"Charlotte's writing beautifully conveys the arduous, yet hopeful reality of living as a neurodivergent individual in a world predominantly designed for non-autistic people. As a professional working within the mental health sector, I have supported clients to feel less alone as they navigate their self or formal diagnosis of ASD, and I truly believe that Charlotte's words will metaphorically embrace these lost individuals, offering guidance and reassurance in times of deep uncertainty. Thank you, Charlotte, for empowering our community with your eloquent words of wisdom."

Emily Hustwick, Autism & Mental Health

Consultant

"Charlotte is my favourite emerging voice on the poetry scene."

Kate Jenkinson, Executive Coach & Business Poet

Too High to Function

Charlotte R Faulconbridge

ISBN: 978-1-7395396-0-3

To my younger self,

I'm sorry.

I'm sorry for not ever seeing your worth. I'm sorry for not believing in you. I'm sorry for writing you off.

But most of all, I'm sorry for not giving you the love you deserved.

I know I cannot fix the things we went through together, but I don't think I'd want to. Even if I could, it is because of that journey that I now have the love to give back to you.

Love, in the shape of this book: this book that I wrote for you, dedicated to you, was inspired to write because of you.

And the best thing of all about that is that it will help many others too.

Contents

Introduction

"You never get a second chance to make a first impression."

It was Oscar Wilde who imparted these words of wisdom unto the world. Unfortunately for me, they're absolutely true.

Another thing that is absolutely true is that I've been dreading writing this introduction. I've been putting it off for weeks – but now that I have finished the rest of this book, this is all that is left to write. They say that people save the best until last, but I wouldn't get your hopes up.

Just in case you missed it, I hate introductions. Why? Because introductions are usually your first impression of something. I'm autistic, and no matter how hard I try, people's first impressions of me are always the same: I'm awkward, socially clumsy, and just a little bit weird.

A first impression implies that you are being exposed to something new for the first time. Unlike the vast majority of the population who find the novelty of newness exciting and appealing, I despise it. For me, the word 'new' means the unknown, the unpredictable, and many other words that start with the letter 'u' that mean similar things... I like to know exactly what's going to happen, when it's going to happen, and how it's going to happen.

I could rationalise my anxiety surrounding this introduction by claiming that this isn't your first impression of my book at all. Technically speaking, your first impression would have been the front cover. Unless you picked up my book, got someone else to rip off the cover and then started reading it, then this is your second first impression. That sort of makes me feel better about it. I think biscuits would make me feel better about it too.

Another reason why I dislike introductions is that they make me feel uncomfortable, because they make me the centre of attention and invite judgement. I don't do well in situations that involve these things. Although to be honest, I don't think I do well in situations that don't involve these things either.

That's it. I'm not going to procrastinate anymore. I'm just going to get this part over and done with as quickly and to the point as possible. As soon as I've had those biscuits.

.jgcdxhgbghggfrdfdgheghetdytshgdhdtdyehgdytg';dxgbh

gggggggggggggggggggggggggggggggg gggggggggggggggggg

gbbbhhhdtcdhfgh*8888ikhuikjjuy huku hjhfg hnbghfjc
,,vnbgffd,km

I'm back. I mistakenly left the lid of my laptop open, and it would appear my cat tried to help me with this project. How thoughtful. (Although, I do hope that means we're not going to be co-authors. I really don't want to have the conversation with my publisher explaining why I need to be paid partly in cash, partly in cat treats.)

Whilst I was gone, I did manage to find a smidge of confidence to actually get on with writing this part. I also found a couple of chocolate hobnobs and half a garibaldi, left desecrated in the depths of the biscuit tin. Why is the key always *confidence*, anyway? Why can't it be social ineptitude and anxiety-induced sweaty palms? I'm great at those things!

I've written most of this book in the middle of the Coronavirus pandemic. I have a weakened immune system, so I've been shielding. This means I got to do what I love the most – stay inside and avoid all close contact with people. For years, people have been trying to get me to broaden my social horizons, but now I've had a justifiable reason why I shouldn't do that – finally, my lifestyle has been legitimised. It makes things a whole lot easier for me. Us autistics invented social distancing years before it was cool.

For me, the pandemic came at the perfect time – just when I started to love myself.[1] I realise that may appear to make absolutely no sense whatsoever. To understand why it *does* make sense, you must first understand a little bit about the autistic brain. Well, my autistic brain.

Up until just a few months before the world plunged into chaos, staying inside would still have been my perfect scenario. But in those short months of blissful calm, in the early spring of 2020, I learned more about my autism than I had ever learned from any medical professional. For the first time I began to see how, in my day-to-day life, I put other people on pedestals, whilst simultaneously belittling myself. I'd held myself hostage to the pressure of constantly feeling like I needed to make others happy by fitting into neurotypical expectations, when I had completely forgotten about the person who really mattered. (Me.)

---

1. Is there such thing as a perfect time for a global disaster? Probably not.

After leaving the structured bubble of school life, I had been trying to navigate life in the real world... when it dawned on me. I was never going to be happy if I kept trying to fit in with my peers or force myself to do what I thought was expected of someone of my age – because guess what? I don't fit in, and I'm never quite going to.

Now I know that isn't a bad thing. My traits make me different, not inadequate. Autism is something that should be celebrated, not commiserated. We deserve to be accepted for who we are, not who we feel we have to be.

When I began to see just how destructive the effects of trying to be someone I wasn't really was, I didn't want to fear my differences anymore. Experiencing the mental and physical impacts of forcing myself to conform was far scarier than anything I could have ever imagined. I didn't care anymore if I was different. That was what made me unique. Other people's opinions no longer mattered to me, and I wasn't going to be banished by their bureaucracy. I just wish that I had come to this realisation sooner – before my life was turned completely upside down.

Even though the process of letting go was painful, and undeniably messy, it was the best thing I have ever done, and I encourage everyone who is in my position to do the same. Not only did I start to discover how to live with my autism, but I also discovered how to love it, and I finally began to see how my autism (and me) could belong in the world.

My first impression of autism is that it is something that will hold you back and stop you achieving your dreams. In a way, I was right – it can be those things... but only if you let it. It took me a long time to see that there are a lot of positive things about my autism; things that I wouldn't have if I was neurotypical: my deeply retentive memory; my appreciation for detail; and my ability to reproduce and play a piece of music just by listening to it... I get to experience the world in a completely different way to everybody else – and it is pure magic.

If I'd have gone into the pandemic without reaching this point in my life, then I'd probably never have come outside again. I would have taken it as a sign, lived my life as a recluse, continue believing that my first impression of the world was the right one: that it wasn't the place for me.

After getting to know Earth for quite some years now, I have concluded that my first impression was incorrect. So, whilst waiting for the apocalypse to blow over, I thought I'd use the time to tell you why I was wrong.

Writing this book has been one big exercise in exposure therapy. Mainly because I don't like talking about myself – ironic, as that is, in fact, the subject of the book. There were moments during writing where specific experiences brought out emotions in me that I had supressed for many years. I never thought I would revisit them with myself, let alone anyone else. Having gone through this freeing and at times painful process, I have seen that vulnerability is a superpower. It allows you to break down the walls in your life, and even release others from the same prisons.

Now, having just said I'm the subject of the book, and although it's written through autobiographical accounts of my most awkward moments, my most challenging conquests, and my most epic existential crises – really, this book *isn't* about me. It's about autism, the power of the mind, and why we should celebrate all of the weird and wonderful things about it. The good, the bad, and the socially ugly!

After years of feeling lost, I no longer feel alone. I have finally found myself, and now all I want to do is to reunite others with their true selves, too. I can't think of anything else I'd rather spend my time doing than raising awareness for neurodiversity. Hopefully, this book will enlighten you about why you should take some time to get to know autism, before judging it on first impressions.

(Note: if you're reading this to try to find out whether you are autistic or not, then I have a simple test for you. I don't mean the kind of test that involves right and wrong answers, but a test of hilarity. If you find yourself laughing at this book without a care in the world, then I think it's fair to say you're neurotypical. If you read my story with the same look of horror that was on my face when I experienced the contents – welcome to the club.)[2]

---

2. If you do happen to find yourself laughing at my expense, just take a minute to remember exactly who you're laughing at. A disabled girl. Don't look so mortified! It's perfectly okay to laugh at me. Why shouldn't you? What makes me so special? Guess I walked straight into that one...

Life on Mars

I may not have gone where I intended to go, but I think I've ended up where I needed to be. [1]

Douglas Adams

Playlist for Chapter 1

Karma Chameleon, Culture Club

Life on Mars? David Bowie

We Don't Have To Take Our Clothes Off, Jermaine Stewart

My Old School, Steely Dan

Homesick, The Cure

Ticket to the Moon, Electric Light Orchestra

Lippy Kids, Elbow

Goodbye Yellow Brick Road, Elton John

Go Your Own Way, Fleetwood Mac

Right. Before I get into this, I should probably warn you that I have a bit of a problem with going off on one. At the moment, I am *trying* to think about how I'm going to start this book, when all I can actually think about are Boeing 747 aeroplanes. I just saw one out of the window. Boeing 747s made their debut in 1969. My mum, Holly, also made her debut in 1969.

Now I'm thinking of holly leaves and how they are symbolic of Christmas, because the Romans sent boughs from the bushes to their friends at this time. Christmas makes me think of the colours red, gold, and green. These colours also feature in the lyrics of Culture Club's 1983 number one hit single, *Karma Chameleon*.[2] The music video for *Karma Chameleon* was set on board a paddle steamer on the Mississippi river just downstream from NASA's largest rocket testing site, the Stennis Space Centre...

(This is how my brain works. I can pretty much guarantee you that it operates differently to yours, and that's because I'm autistic.)

...The engine in the Apollo 11 space shuttle was tested at the Stennis Space Centre, and exactly 74 days after my mum was born, NASA sent three men to the surface of the moon. One of the

---

2. Fun Fact: My gran's cousin wrote this song; he was the keyboard player in Culture Club!

major companies who helped manufacture the components of this spacecraft was *Boeing*. And just like that, we've gone full circle – and we're right back to me sitting at my computer, figuring out how to start this book, and trying not to get distracted by what model of aeroplane is flying in the sky visible outside my window.

This is how my mind goes from one thing to another, constantly creating connections and patterns. I have a diagnosis of Asperger's Syndrome, a form of 'high-functioning' autism. This is quite possibly the most inaccurate name for my diagnosis – because I definitely do not function *highly*. Yes, I can bore you to near-death over Einstein's theory of relativity and his mathematical construct of space-time, but I can't go into a café and order my own food; have a conversation over the phone; or leave the house without completing one of my many routines.

Just like a computer, I have a processor running my system. Except my processor was taken from a computer that was built in 1981. It's incredible at storing random pieces of information, but it's also incredibly slow. That is why I find situations that involve quick responses, like conversations, difficult. It's hard to keep up in a world where everybody else's software is fully up to date, when mine is running on a whole other operating system.

One of the reasons why my processor is so slow is because my brain has to consciously absorb and store every piece of information that it receives. All of my senses are heightened, making the most mundane of tasks difficult to complete. Every colour, texture, smell, taste and sound have to be examined in minutiae. It feels like my brain is holding a magnifying glass up to the universe; not only does it magnify the good, but the bad is intensified too. It's exhausting, irritating, and worst of all, completely out of my control.

To add to the fact that my software isn't up to date, it is also prone to glitches. These glitches occur when I'm being hurried to do something that I'm not ready for, if I've not been given clear enough instructions, or when I'm taken too far out of my comfort zone. Sometimes, if too many glitches occur in a short space of time, it can cause a system malfunction that will force my computer to shut down.

In this situation, the usual response is to simply get angry with the computer. People come along and try to fix it. They think that by poking every button and screaming loudly, that will somehow solve the problem. But a computer *can't* calm down and reboot again if someone is prodding every key and shaking the screen. And what if the computer was never broken in the first place, therefore it doesn't need 'fixing'?

I was diagnosed as autistic nearly a decade ago, when I was fifteen.

I would have expected that the moments leading up to and immediately after my diagnosis to be monumental. And they were, but not in the negative way I had imagined. Instead, and rather unexpectedly, I felt a huge sense of relief. I felt free. It was possibly the best day of my life. For as long as I can remember, I had always felt different. Not different in a cool, trendy, edgy sort of way – different in an odd, genetic, psychological sort of way. The kind of 'different' that doesn't quite have the same ring to it.

When I was younger, I felt so out of place in the world that I continually asked my mum if I was adopted. I just couldn't believe that I could be in any way related to my family; I was convinced there had been some terrible mix up at the stork crèche, between two identical brown-eyed, mousy-haired baby girls. Sometimes, I didn't even feel remotely human. I felt completely alienated. Something just didn't seem to fit about me being on this planet. I used to lie in bed and look up at the stars outside my window, wondering which one I came from.

I couldn't help but feel sorry for the girl that the stork mixed me up with – she probably hated Mars! It's quiet, and apparently has a lack of atmosphere (due, I guess, to the fact there are no people), which makes it prime autistic real estate. Its moons are Phobos and Deimos, named after the sons of the Greek god of war. Their names translate into English as Fear and Panic – fitting, as fear and panic sort of sum up how I feel a lot of the time.

Even though I can't deny I would have loved it up there, I'd have had to do an awful lot of redecorating. Red just isn't my colour. (And it couldn't have been all bad for the girl stranded on Mars; after all, David Bowie did write a song about her...) And then, I got my diagnosis –the proof I needed that I *was* in fact human, and not some previously undiscovered alien life form.[3]

Autism was the reason I had always felt this way, and my diagnosis really helped to explain things for me: why the things I disliked were always the things that everybody else seemed to love. I soon found out that I wasn't alone. It turns out, there are loads of us. Whole colonies of autistic people sent to try and bring order to a planet that reigns in chaos. Our mission is far from over though, as the species that inhabit planet Earth seem to enjoy all things rebellious. They don't seem to care if their knives and forks aren't exactly two centimetres away from the edge of the table, or if they set the volume on their televisions to a number other than a multiple of five. In fact, they don't seem to have any form of

---

3. Although, my brain does come with medical and legal documentation, which could easily make it an X file.

structure to their lives at all. Quite honestly, I don't know how they've made it this far. They definitely couldn't have survived this long without us.

I can't leave my bedroom until my blinds are exactly twenty centimetres above my window ledge.[4] If my blinds are wonky, will they skew the balance of the universe? Is it a matter of life or death? Well, I'm still alive, so I think that gives me a sufficient argument to suggest that it is. Even if it isn't, I'm not going to start risking it now. That would be utterly frivolous.

Like most people, my knowledge of autism used to be fairly limited. Before being diagnosed, I thought that having autism meant that you were either a sociopathic mastermind like Sherlock Holmes, or that you belonged to the cast of *Rain Man*. The first doctor I ever saw about getting a diagnosis categorically told me that I couldn't possibly be autistic, because I had such a deep understanding of empathy and that I was 'too pretty'.

Autistic people are either seen as total geniuses or complete burdens on society – there doesn't seem to be a middle ground.

---

4. Yes, I do always keep a ruler on my window ledge. I keep two in fact. My favourite one and then a spare, just in case anything happens to the favourite. I know it's bad to have favourites, but I don't think the rulers mind.

The terms high and low functioning are incredibly inaccurate. People often assume that because I'm classed as 'high functioning', it means that I don't struggle as much as other people on the spectrum. The truth is, some days I can function reasonably well, but depending on my energy and anxiety levels, on others I can barely function at all. Sometimes, I can be *too* high functioning for my own good, as I often struggle to keep up with my brain's processing. (Too high to function, maybe?)

Conversely, it's also often assumed that because I have a neurological condition, I cannot think for myself or make my own decisions – but I have a brain, just like everyone else. Granted, it is a different brain, maybe even an entirely different breed of brain altogether, but just because I'm quiet and introverted doesn't mean that I don't have a lot to say.

Just to be clear, I am definitely not a genius, and if you were to drop a packet of toothpicks on the floor, I couldn't instantaneously tell you how many there were. Sorry. I'm just one of the regular ones. You know, without any superpowers.

Because autism is classed as an invisible disability, it makes it hard to detect and understand. If I were missing a leg, there'd be no problem.[5] You'd know exactly what was wrong and how to help. When people tell me that I don't *look* autistic, I can't help but feel like they are slightly disappointed. I really don't know what they were expecting to see. Horns and a tail, maybe?

At least that feeling of disappointment is quickly overshadowed by a different feeling – this time, confusion – because apparently, we can sometimes seem 'too normal' to be autistic. Ahh yes, time for my least favourite word. We do seem so *normal* don't we? In fact, we're just like you! Scary right?

You neurotypicals have kind of started to make me feel bad. Some of you think that us Auties are like rare breeds of undiscovered creatures that are yet to be featured on a David Attenborough documentary. We are just people too, you know.

And there are some that will think I shouldn't feel bad, as apparently everyone is 'a little bit autistic'. Sort of like how someone can be 'a little bit pregnant'.[6]

---

5. Technically there would be a problem, but that's not the point I'm trying to make here.

6. Like that's possible.

Others may even call me inspirational, and you know what? Yes, I bloody am! I can totally see why having a blue badge and getting to park closer to Sainsbury's would give me a title so deserving of the word.

Over the years, I've come to see that autistic people are as varied and individual as everyone else. While we do have some traits in common, those shared traits may be expressed in completely different ways. I'll gladly be the first one to admit to having fallen into the trap of believing the many stereotypes. The truth is, the only way to truly understand autism is to *ask people who are autistic.*

There is no right or wrong way to be autistic either. If you have met just one individual with autism, then that really does mean that you have met just one individual with autism. The reason it's called the 'autism spectrum' is because everyone on it experiences the world differently. I appreciate that this makes it hard to put into words, which is inconvenient, considering that I have decided to write a book about it.

Autism is a neurological processing disorder. All that means is that our brains are wired to receive and interpret information differently. Sort of like if you were to hire an amateur electrician to do your electrics, only to find that when he'd gone, he'd put all the wires back in completely the wrong places.

Our processing time is much longer, because the information we are trying to receive doesn't always go to the right place. Imagine you had to walk all the way to the kitchen and back, every time you wanted to turn on your bedroom light. These complications are why we struggle to function like everybody else. If we have to walk to the opposite end of the house just to flick the right switch, we can't keep up. It's exhausting as it sounds. And if that wasn't challenging enough, then imagine having to try and remember which switch corresponds to the correct light in each room, when all of your wires are crossed.

Aside from these complications, being autistic can be truly amazing. We are intelligent, strongly focused and incredibly creative. If our strengths are channelled correctly, then they can easily compensate for the challenges we face daily. But if those challenges overwhelm us and start to take over, it can be easy to lose sight of our potential. And yes, there is *great* potential. Albert Einstein, Mozart, and Sir Isaac Newton were just some of the masterminds considered to be on the spectrum, and what fantastic footsteps to follow in!

In every educational or social setting, I always felt isolated. I was the odd one out; the puzzle piece that just somehow didn't seem to fit. Looking back, it started to dawn on me as far back as nursery. I noticed that everyone else would play with their toys actively, moving them around, crashing into each other; creatively playing with toys in a way that didn't seem realistic to me, such as making action men ride unicorns. The other children would all laugh, smile, and yell excitedly.

Silently and expressionless, I would spend hours meticulously lining up my toys. There was nothing chaotic about my displays of fun. I have always been realistic, so mixing up superheroes with mythical creatures just wasn't right. (I find the very concept of superheroes *existing* a troubling one in the first place.)

One day, another child accidentally ran through my statuesque display, and I had a complete internal collapse. I screamed the place down. I remember rushing to the toilets and was compelled to repeatedly bang my head on one of the cubicle doors, just so I could unleash my frustration at the lack of order in my creation. A few years later, I asked Father Christmas to bring me a morse code tapper, an electronic toothbrush, and a dimmer switch – that I unknowingly used as fidget gadgets.

I guess toys meant something different for me.

Growing up in a world where being anything other than ordinary wasn't acceptable, I was in the minority. Naturally, we think that whoever is in the majority must be right, and when you're being personally attacked on a daily basis for *just being you*, you start to blame yourself. When every difference, quirk and trait is perceived to be a flaw, you can only stand accused and presume it's all your fault. I was struggling to survive in a society that just wasn't built for me.

At home, surrounded by my family who understood me, I didn't seem to be all that unusual. But surrounded by my peers, my differences became much more apparent, simply because I was constantly being compared and judged – by myself and others.

As we become teenagers, we begin to establish our own sense of identity, and these differences only get greater, and more troublesome to navigate.

By this time, most of my friends had started discovering makeup, hair rollers, and push-up bras, but I couldn't really care less about what I looked like as a 14-year-old. Even now, as long as I feel comfortable, that's all that matters to me. I'd happily go to Tesco's in my dressing gown and slippers. I'm 23, and I have only *just* tried using a pair of hair straighteners. (Ironically, they used to belong to my ex-boyfriend, so even men are apparently more in touch with their feminine side than I am.)

Looking 'good' didn't improve my functionality as a human; and as a technique to attract members of the opposite sex? Only useful if you want that kind of attention in the first place. Physical contact isn't what drives me. I'd happily live my life without ever touching another human being. It seems as though I was born without any of the natural human instincts to procreate and to replenish the Earth's stock. Sex is an entirely mental process for me. There's not much about the outer appearance of a human that will ever make me blush, as to me, the sexiest organ is the brain. Having a larger-than-average temporal lobe might just be the only thing that really gets me going. If I can't find someone that stimulates my cerebral cortex, they have very little chance of stimulating anything else.

But my friends didn't understand any of this, and it became an ongoing rift that eventually divided us. I tried my best to fit in, but in doing so, I found myself being forced into living up to neurotypical expectations, such as going to parties, getting drunk and sleeping with every boy I came into contact with. The truth is,

I'd rather stay at home and play the piano, read a book, or watch the snooker.

I thought that by forcing myself to conform to neurotypical expectations, I would somehow fix all the pieces of me that seemed to be broken. But I only broke more hearts in the process, including my own.

Till recently, I spent my life beating myself up over the fact that I wasn't the way society dictated I should be. According to society's rules, by now I should be able to drive, have a university degree, and be able to live independently. It didn't ever occur to me that there is a very good reason why I couldn't do these things as easily as my peers. And it's taken me a long time to realise that these things didn't define my self-worth.

It's fair to say that school almost destroyed me. The mainstream approach to education just wasn't made for people who didn't fit inside 'the box'. I had been able to mask my way through, coping, until I began secondary school. This is when our futures really start to depend on our performance, and when all pressure was intensified, especially at a private school. Over the next five years of my school life, despite my classwork being excellent, my end of year exam results began a continual and significant decline. When I was on the cusp of taking my GCSE qualifications, it was down to the wire as to whether I would receive adequate support and appropriate exam provisions.

I couldn't see that the prejudice and negligence I received from most of the staff and students wasn't my fault, but due to a total lack of awareness of people who had a disability. The resistance to offer me minimal inclusion or educational support made me feel like I wasn't worthy of help. What was I supposed to do? Stay at home and hide away like some monster? (That's exactly what I ended up doing.)

I have always loved the principle of school. I love learning, expanding my knowledge, and knowing *why*. I don't even care much about what subject I happen to be learning. I just enjoy discovering new fascinations about our world, and building a new shelf in my brain on which to store that information.

From a young age, we are taught that our whole lives depend on passing our exams. They say that without a degree, we won't be successful or be able to have a fulfilled life of any kind. Well, they did at my school anyway. I tortured myself with that pressure for the duration of my school career. In the end, school made my life so difficult that I could no longer attend. I felt unwelcome, I was being pushed out – all because the support I required felt like it was too much effort to implement. I felt like my life had ended before it had even begun.

I had been brainwashed into thinking that essentially, it would all be over if I didn't get my A-Levels and go to university. Yet the establishment that thrust this ideology onto me was the very same one that wasn't prepared to meet my needs and see my education through – the education that my mum was working full time to pay for. To hear that the Head would rather forgo thousands of pounds a year than accommodate me made me question my entire self-worth. Did I not deserve the same opportunities as my peers, just because I needed clear instructions, rest breaks, have the lights in the classroom ever so slightly dimmed, and to be seated next to the door so I didn't feel claustrophobic?

My plan had been to get all my grades and then go to university like everybody else, preferably Manchester, where I would get a First in Astrophysics, and a post-grad job at Hawaii's observatory on the island of Mauna Kea, away from the plague that is humanity, where I could be at one with the natural world.

Mauna Kea is one of the few places on the planet that inhabits a specific breed of sea algae; at night, the coast comes alive with the hue of electric blue due to natural bioluminescence. Against the stark cobalt sea, a fiery furnace, spitting and spewing for attention, lies dormant on the mountainside. I would sit and watch the waves break upon the shore, shattering against one another, flicking millions of shards of light into the ether. I'd turn on my telescope, and one by one, watch the stars being switched on.

But someone else got my degree. Someone else got my job. Even if I had continued torturing myself by trying to fit into mainstream education, I was nowhere near ready to leave home. Home has always been my safe place, and the thought of being shoved into student housing with a bunch of complete strangers is not something I'd ever want to sign myself up to.

This was an unrealistic prospect to require of myself at the time. I'd only recently been diagnosed, and I was still in the early stages of learning about what it meant to be autistic. Instead of being continually thrust into mainstream schooling, I needed to seek out specialised education that could support my needs. My brain is wired in a completely different way, so obviously, it can't function in the same way as everyone else's. Frankly, I don't know why I ever expected it to.

...Actually, I do know why.

I was in denial. I didn't *want* to be different. I didn't want to have to take regular rest breaks from my lessons or have things explained to me in a particular way so I would understand them better. I wanted to think and learn in the exact same way that everyone else thought and learnt. I had been conditioned into thinking that being different was wrong, and I couldn't face watching my friends go off and living their lives. They were free now; free to go anywhere their hearts desired. I suppose the clincher for me was that they had *always* been free, they just hadn't realized the extent of it till now – they weren't impounded within the limits of their own minds.

Even the shitty things about becoming an adult, like working, paying taxes, and contributing to society... I wanted those things as well, not just the good bits. I just wanted to live in the real world. Not in a bubble.

'The world is your oyster!' 'As long as you work hard you can achieve anything!' Well, it turns out that you need a lot more than shellfish and inspirational quotes to achieve your goals in life, if it hasn't been that kind to you. I was only sixteen, but I already felt like I had failed. Failed at life, failed at being a human, and failed at being happy. I foolishly thought that just being those three things was easy.

I found that the only way I could deal with the situation at the time was to pretend that my friends didn't exist. Shortly after I left school, despite having received the exam provisions I needed (not without a fight) which enabled me to pass my GCSEs with all As and A stars, I broke down. I realised that having a piece of paper with sparkling results meant absolutely nothing if I couldn't act on it. I chucked my phone in a drawer, changed the locks to my mind and threw away the key. It was like I completely dropped off the face of the Earth. I wanted to pretend that I didn't exist. Besides, I thought that's what most people wanted anyway.

The saddest part was that I wasn't missed at all. In theory, I'd gotten what I wanted... but had I? I hadn't understood until that moment just how distant I had become from the people I once called friends. This realisation further reinforced my retreat into my bedroom, drawing the curtains, listening to the drones of Robert Smith on repeat. In the back of my mind, I had always feared that there wasn't a place for me out there, and now it seemed to have been confirmed.

There is a deeper state of despair, beneath the layers of rage, depression, and guilt. A place where no human mind should be left to wander. Under all the pain lies a no man's land of human emotion. It is barren, empty, and derelict; a place where you forget how to feel. Where the fighting stops, and you begin to flatline. Nothing matters to you anymore. You become nothing more than an observer.

To be able to feel something, to be able to think and wonder is what makes us as a species so unique in our vast universe. Whether what you feel is sadness or joy, we all have that powerful ability. But *not to feel anything,* to be sterilised from opinion and passion, is more frightening than ever feeling pain. As long as you feel *something,* no matter how unpleasant, you know that you're alive.

I was being engulfed by my emptiness. Gravity asserted its grip, pulling me down, and that black hole was devouring my soul, one day at a time. I felt like phoning up NASA and asking them if they could stop the world so I could get off. Besides, why just pretend you don't exist, when you could actually wipe yourself out from existence altogether?

The moment that changed me was when even *that* didn't go to plan. How do you know it didn't go to plan? Because I'm sitting here telling you it didn't. This was when my journey really began. I realised that I didn't actually want to leave Earth. I had just simply forgotten how to *feel.*

Holding onto anger and resentment is like cutting your own wrists and expecting someone else to feel the pain. When we get into that cycle, all we keep doing is hurting ourselves, for something that someone else did. My resentment of my peers' happiness came from a place of disdain for myself. But you cannot hate your way to love. The vision I held of myself in my head had to change, if I was ever to have a chance of being happy.

Being autistic wasn't my fault, and it was no one else's either, because it wasn't a 'fault'. But refusing to treat someone with a little bit of respect and dignity for something that they cannot change about themselves – that is faulty. The very problem of being human is that we judge ourselves from our interior, and everyone else from their exteriors. If you ask me, that isn't a very fair system.

There is no definitive and precise formula that you can whack out to fit your exact trauma, as everyone's healing process is different. But choosing to start the process of letting go is a good first step. Even if that means you begin without closure, an apology, or justice.

The First Law of Thermodynamics states that the energy in our universe can be neither destroyed nor created. Everything in it is made up of energy: the clouds, the stars, every single living thing. We are all fundamentally made up from the very same particles that radiated out from when our universe was created, nearly 14 billion years ago. Over the millions of years in a star's lifetime, a star will create all of the elements that we depend on for life on Earth. Our chemical ingredients were cooked in the hearts of these ancient stars by the process of nuclear fusion, spat out by explosive supernovae and mixed back into the universe again, only to eventually be forged back together to form galaxies and planets by the relentless pull of gravity.

Every single atom of calcium in our bones, iron we walk on in the ground, and oxygen that we breathe was born in the heart of a dying star. We're quite literally made from stardust. These stars lived hard and died young, and we are part of a cycle where life is reborn from the ashes of the old. When we die, the elements and particles that make up our beings are returned to the universe to refuel our cosmic story.

Over the many decades of space exploration, in the search for new worlds like our home planet, there is only one place that we know of where life exists. Just one, in over 125 billion galaxies, each containing trillions of stars, where collections of atoms are able to form beings that can comprehend the beauty of it all.

The probability that you're even sitting here reading this book right now is 1 in $10^{2,685,000}$. That's 10 followed by 2,685,000 zeros. Your chances of existing are basically none. So, trust me, the very fact you exist makes you worthy in the first place. Self-love, self-respect, self-worth – there's a reason why they all start with the self. You can't find them anywhere else.

This law of physics, this story of the origins of life is what helps me, when I drift back to how I used to think about myself; back when I thought I was broken. Little did I know that there was more than one way to get through life. I wish they'd teach you that at school, because nothing is good, bad, ugly, or beautiful, until you compare it. You don't have to take the same path as everybody else. You always have a choice. You can go your own way.

There was a time when I thought that I'd never be able to get a degree or a job, but now I know that I'm more than capable. I just have to achieve those things in a slightly different way to most people. A way that's better for me, at my own pace, that I'll be able to cope with. It'll be like taking a different route on a journey but reaching the exact same destination.

Sometimes it can be really difficult to accept that there will be things that you cannot do unsupported, because of your disability. Even if you're *not* autistic, being human is hard, and we all have our limits. While it is painful to accept when we can't always do things as easily as everyone else, it's even more painful to continuously set yourself up for failure, by holding onto expectations that you cannot live up to.

I realise now that completing my education with the correct support for my needs has enabled me to enhance my growth, not diminish it. Being able to accept that help was not without its challenges – but it has helped me unlock my true potential.

It seems counterintuitive, but I'm having to un-learn a lot about what I thought it meant to be human. The more we insist on loving exactly who we are, the more we resist the constructs that society has laid down in front of us. The more we resist, the more we unmask our authentic selves, and the less we care about fitting in and pleasing others.

I left school just over five years ago. In that time, I've met some truly inspiring people who have helped me uncover my true potential. They've made me realise that autism was never to blame; people's expectations of how I should be living my life were at the root of my unhappiness. Looking back, I now know that there were lots of things that I could have done to help myself get out of that all-consuming black hole. I didn't know what those things were at the time. But now I do, and I'm stronger for it. I hope you will be, too.

You may be wondering whether I am writing this book in Hawaii after all. You probably want me to tell you that there is a happy ending, and that I'm finally out there living my dream. That narrative would probably sell better, but it's not the truth. I'm not living the high life in Hawaii, and I'm not living that dream. But I am more grounded than I have ever been. It *is* a happy ending. Happier than I could have ever imagined.

Every time you look up at the sky, you become a time traveller. Light from the sun takes eight minutes to reach Earth. Light from the star Sirius takes eight years to reach us, which means if you go outside and look at Sirius tonight, you will see it how it appeared eight years ago.

Looking up at the Andromeda galaxy (the most distant celestial object we can see from Earth with the naked eye), the light you're seeing is 2.5 million years old. Every time we look at Andromeda, we're seeing it before humans ever existed.

As we look further into the cosmos, we travel further back in time. All of the light that we can see scattered across the sky is merely the ghost of what happened millions and millions of years ago. It's as if all of time and space was on one giant film reel, being laced into a giant film projector. Every star a light source and every shadow a shutter. As each frame of film is moved in rapid succession across the sky, the stars flicker and twinkle, to reveal one of the best movies ever made.[7]

Those small moments of happiness that are barely experienced are the ones that are the most magnificent. Those serendipitous seconds, walking home in the early hours, tipsily singing Britpop to wheelie bins and flowers whilst the dawn is breaking, or rolling over in bed to see your loved one sound asleep – they are the moments that truly transcend. Finding joy in the little things doesn't make you any less ambitious; it merely makes you more grateful and present in the moment.

You cannot rush progress. The stars won't suddenly be unplugged from the mains. Nor will the moonglow stop lighting up the night. Waves will continue to break, and volcanoes will continue to threaten. To be able to appreciate the beauty and wonder of the island of Hawaii, I first needed to find that feeling without it.

Some people seem to be obsessed with progress – they feel like they must rush through time without shaking its hands, and speed through lists of people to meet and places to see – so much so that sometimes, they forget to actually look. Perhaps it's down to the absurdity and naivety of youth, but I think that to be unafraid of

---

7. Except when it's cloudy.

life, you have to live it taking all the time in the world. I am not afraid anymore. As long as you live every moment with passion and presence, none of it will be wasted.

As important as it is to learn from the past, the present is where I found myself, and the future is where I will live.

I realised that my passion for space was born from an inherently unhealthy origin. Specifically: my bed. Even more specifically: at night, when I would gaze into the void outside my window, trying to work out which world I really belonged to. I've come to realise that to appreciate other worlds, you must first learn to appreciate your own.

To answer that desperate question from my younger self – the question of where I belonged – I shouldn't have been looking back through time. I needed to be looking right where I was.

The Phantom of the Operative

The best and most beautiful things in the world cannot be seen or even touched – they must be felt with the heart.

Helen Keller

Playlist for Chapter 2

You'll Always Find Me In The Kitchen At Parties, Jona Lewie

The Phantom Of the Opera, Andrew Lloyd Webber

Ghost Town, The Specials

Computer Love, Kraftwerk

When You Say Nothing At All, Ronan Keating

Canary In A Coalmine, The Police

Alone Again (Naturally), Gilbert O'Sullivan

That's Not Her Style, Billy Joel

I would just like to take a moment to acknowledge how well I've done so far with writing this book, considering that English isn't my first language. My first language is Autism. Music is my second, followed in third place by Cat.

Communication isn't a term that's bound by the spoken word; people have been communicating without speaking for centuries. Before the rise of modern technology, if you wanted to send an email, you had to write a letter. If you wanted to post a tweet, you had to train up a homing pigeon. Now we are able to interact with whomever we want, whenever we want, instantly, at the push of a button. And more importantly, without having to speak.

Verbal communication isn't something that comes naturally to autistic people. One theory behind this is that we don't get neurologically rewarded by social interactions. Most people get a hit of dopamine when making eye contact or having a conversation. But there is evidence to suggest that us Auties don't get the chemical release that makes neurotypical people enjoy socialising. Therefore, it's important that you don't force social interaction upon us, as it's something we aren't necessarily wired to excel in. It must be something we want to do on our own terms.

Some autistic people are happier staying in a world of their own and will often thrive without the interference of others. This was me for a long time.

I was quite happy keeping myself to myself and not getting involved in social situations. This was mainly because the amount of concentration required to be able to hold a decent level of conversation seemed to suck all the fun out of it. I found talking more of a chore than a source of contentment. But then – I discovered parties. You might think that on the whole, a party is an autistic person's nightmare, and you would be absolutely right: the noise; the unnecessary amount of people; the spreading of various diseases via a selection of hors d'oeuvres...

However, after being pressured into attending a friend's 18th birthday party, I discovered the one saving grace of these social gatherings. *Most people attending them will probably be drunk.* This means that the likelihood of them remembering anything you say is fairly limited, so it doesn't matter if what you say is considered awkward.

At this very party, one of my other friends was quite ill in front of me. Overall, it wasn't the most pleasant of situations, but after he was sick into the kitchen sink, he looked up at me, and for the first time in my life I made eye contact with someone who felt more uncomfortable about it than I did. I had a splendiferous moment, when – for just a few minutes – I thought I had finally cracked all socialisation, and that I should have a lot more interactions with people who are drunk to the point of vomiting.

I don't drink – partly because I don't like the idea of losing control, but mainly because I have a hard time communicating *without* the interference of alcohol, so I don't think inebriation would do me any favours.

It's the same with drugs. Apart from loss of control, one of the common side effects of drugtaking is becoming paranoid and anxious. I'm already reaping those benefits without having to take anything, so for me it would be a total waste of money.

Unfortunately, most people don't go around living their lives in a permanent state of drunkenness, so I continued to avoid social interactions as much as possible. Avoiding social situations is a skill I acquired fairly easily. If someone asked me to go the cinema at the weekend, I'd just make up some excuse about having to attend my brother's friend's aunty's sister-in-law's fish's funeral.[1]

---

1. It was an extremely tragic death. I just cannot face going into details.

I bet that everyone has done this at least once, to get out of a social engagement – autistic or not. Whether you've suddenly fallen ill or had to wash your hair, we've all been there. But there was one day when I perhaps went too far with an excuse for why I couldn't possibly talk to another human being. The human being in question, a delivery operative, arriving at my doorstep carrying a cardboard box and a newspaper, with a degree-level qualification in persistent doorbell ringing.

There is never a dull moment when living in a house populated by a family of five humans (whose ages span from 23 to 83) that is also home to three owls, four cats and a couple of dogs. But on those rare occasions when the house is empty of other people, it's down to me and the menagerie to hold the fort.

Normally when I hear the doorbell ring, I simply ignore it. A few seconds will pass, and whoever is delivering our industrial-sized bag of pet food and copy of 'What Has Humanity Done to Eff Up the World Today?' kindly leaves the goods on the doorstep. But there came a day when this didn't happen.

I had just settled into the silence of a human-free house, only to be unsettled by the ringing of the doorbell. Our delivery man knows the drill. Ring the doorbell, try to avoid being deafened by the barks of overexcited dogs, and if no one appears, leave the pet food and the newspaper on the doorstep. Then exit, pursued by a cat's glare.

But this was not the usual delivery man. It was his younger and much more enthusiastic successor. He *didn't* know the drill. Instead of ringing the bell, resisting the possible long-term effects of a dog's bark on the eardrum, leaving the pet food and the paper on the doorstep, then vacating the area whilst being watched by a half-asleep cat – he rang the bell and didn't seem to give a damn about the perforation of one's lughole, as when no one appeared, he kept ringing.

All I could do was take comfort in the fact that he couldn't stay ringing my doorbell forever. He had his whole life ahead of him. Thousands of other bells that needed to be rung. [23]

---

2. He had worked through the ranks of bell ringing when he started life as a Morris dancer. Then he became familiar with the bells that tinkle when entering and exiting a corner shop. Some might say he became too familiar with them, as he was later arrested for shoplifting. As he got himself back on the straight and narrow, after his dancing days had nearly pushed him over the edge, he realised that bell ringing was what he was destined to do. So, he became a delivery man. Licenced to ding-a-ling-a-ling, all day-a-ling-a-long. But his dream, a dream shared amongst many bell ringers, is to ring a much bigger, and more important bell, like Big Ben. There is tough competition in bell ringing though, so if that career path didn't work out, he could always branch out into door knocking. There is far less competition with knocking these days. He could have his pick: Big Ben, St Pauls Cathedral, Westminster Abbey. Although I think he would prefer the latter, as apparently Abbey in Westminster had the best knockers in town.

3. What? I did warn you right at the start of this book that I could go off on one at any given moment. Don't look so surprised.

Thankfully the ringing eventually came to an end, so I assumed that he'd left. The dogs were docile, the cats were content. Peace and tranquillity had been restored. I got up from the sofa, only to turn around and see a face. The face of the campanologist, peering at me through the window. I froze. I didn't want him to think that I'd been deliberately ignoring him and wasting his time. Well, I suppose I had, but not out of rudeness or disrespect. I just couldn't face opening the door to talk to somebody that I had never met before. The prospect of talking to a stranger is one that fills me with dread, fear, and that 'I'm going to be violently sick any second' feeling. I struggle enough talking to people that I *have* met before.

He looked confused, and his cheeks were coloured with a pink hue that Dulux might call 'Slightly Pissed Off'. If I wasn't willing to open the door before I saw his face, I definitely wasn't going to open it now. Before I even had the chance to panic, the embers in my brain suddenly sparked. I had had my most ingenious idea to date.

I was going to pretend to be dead.

It was perfect. You can't be pissed off with a dead body, let alone talk to one. There was however, just one major flaw in this plan: I was already standing up. I've never seen a dead body in the flesh, but I'm pretty sure they are usually horizontal. This didn't hold me back though, as I had yet another brain wave.

A ghost! Of course! It was the obvious option available to me at the time. Not only was I the right orientation to be a ghost, but I just so happened to be wearing the right costume. I had on a white lace summer dress and my hair was still damply tousled from washing it earlier. All in all, this gave me the look of a young Victorian girl who had tragically died whilst participating in some water-based activity.[4]

I was vertical. I was wearing the costume. All that was left for me to do was to play the part of the young and soggy Victorian. This role required me to look horrifically ill and to stay as still as possible whilst hauntingly staring at the bellringer through the window. All in all, these responses are quite typical of how I react to meeting a stranger for the first time, so there was actually very little acting involved.

---

4. I didn't have time to do an in-depth character analysis on young-Victorian-girl-who-tragically-died-whilst-participating-in-some-water-based-activity, but I suppose she could have met her fate whilst accidentally stabbing herself whilst doing the washing up. Or jet skiing.

Now, I'm not exactly sure what was going through the delivery man's head at the time, or if he was scared in any way. If he *was* scared, he had forgotten to let his face know how he was feeling. Perhaps he was so frightened that his body had been shocked into a state of paralysis. I soon found out that this wasn't the case as he knocked on the window, held the bag of pet food up to the glass and pointed at the door.[5]

It was a nice try, but he wasn't going to get me to give up that easily. Like any great actress, I just had to commit to my role. I thought it was going rather well, especially when he stopped pointing at the door. This could have been due to the fact I had started to slowly lumber towards the window whilst resting my head completely on my shoulder as if it were hanging from my neck by a couple of torn tendons.

That was the moment he shoved the parcel onto the doorstep. He'd got the message. It was Harry Truman who said if you can't convince them, confuse them. I knew I'd done one or the other, I just wasn't sure which. Whether I'd terrified him or not, he gave up the ghost.

---

5. I saw he had already begun to consider his career in knocking after all.

The delivery man swiftly made his exit, pursued by a scare. If there was anything to learn from this haunting, it was that if no one answers the bell, cut out the middle-Victorian-ghost-girl and just leave the parcel on the doorstep.

I never saw that delivery man again. I wasn't entirely sure why he didn't come back – he knew the drill now. And although I proved how successful playing dead can be in keeping unwarranted socialising at bay, I hadn't yet realised that my methods may have some complicated consequences further down the line...

I like to think that I have grown as a person since this haunting event. Now I try and challenge myself to actively socialise more. This was a decision I made only *when I was ready to do so*. Autistic people aren't born with the social instincts that everyone else has. Naturally speaking, I have the eye contact of an embarrassed Hugh Grant and the vocal expression of a shipping forecast presenter in a trance, so I have had to learn my social cues from scratch, copying others. This comes with plenty of trial and error, so choose whom you wish to be influenced by wisely.

If you're autistic and you've had a bad social experience, it's important to remember that there are people out there who do understand. I promise they exist. Even though I've started to enjoy socialising more, it has to be completely on my terms, with people I trust. Sometimes – in order to *find* people I could trust – I had to let them trust me too. This is called mutual vulnerability. That doesn't mean that you should dive straight in at the deep end and admit to that homicide you got away with last weekend, but just showing a small amount of openness can help people to feel more relaxed around you. As we learned from my previous anecdote, if you look scared to death, then people might be scared to talk to you.[6]

There are two reasons why I didn't used to particularly enjoy socialising. The first reason is that I didn't really like people. The second is that I didn't really like going out.

(*Not really liking people*) + (*Not really liking going out*) = *Not really liking going out with people*

Not off to a great start, I know.

---

6. I've also found that if you bring snacks with you to meet new people, this is an excellent ice breaker. I suppose these are the fundamentals of bribery, but so what?

Over the years, I have been able to dissect my reasons behind not really liking either of these things, and it's not as black and white as it seems. The truth is: people scare me. *Especially* the 'normal' ones. It's stereotypical to think that autistic people show no empathy when it comes to people's feelings, but whenever I talk to someone, whether it's for the first or the hundredth time, all I can think about is *not* upsetting them. I'm terrified by the idea of unintentionally making someone distressed or annoyed, as I'm fully aware that my autistic brain works in its own mysterious ways.

To understand my fear of people, you must first understand the basis of all human social interactions. People aren't fundamentally good or bad. They are just fundamentally people. As a species, this is what makes us unpredictable.

Tech pioneers Steve Jobs and Bill Gates have both been the subject of speculation in terms of being on the autistic spectrum, due to their perceived lack of social skills. These men co-founded two of the most influential technological companies of the twenty first century, Apple and Microsoft.

I can totally understand why Steve Jobs and Bill Gates decided to live their lives in a virtual world, uninhabited by people. They probably found that a world made up of numbers and symbols was a lot easier to understand. Similarly, I find it easier to explain our own metaphysics with actual physics.

The language of computers is similar to the language of maths. In maths, you are either right or wrong; there are only definitive answers. Unfortunately, people aren't quite as simple as that.

In a world where there are seven billion of us, all of whom are different, what is considered to be the right answer for one person might be the wrong answer for someone else. Before you think it, I know there are lots of different computers in existence too – but unlike computers, people don't come with an instruction manual. Which is a bit careless, if you ask me, as I've found that people are a lot more temperamental. At least if you upset a computer, you know exactly where you are; if you piss it off, you know about it.

You can't simply turn someone off and on again, in the hope that their hard drive will be erased after you told your friend they looked a lot fatter in the very expensive dress they just bought compared to their old one that resembled a lab coat. I suppose this is why Auties have a reputation for being rude. Most people have some kind of inbuilt filter that stops the brutal truth slipping through the cracks. If you're autistic, you still have a filter, but it's about as efficient at holding in the truth as a colander is at holding in water. This is why we have the potential to say so many 'wrong' things, one after another, consecutively, in a row. Unlike Piers Morgan, we never actually intend to be rude. It's just how our brains work. Personally, I don't call it rudeness. I call it honesty.

If I'm tired, then I tend to become less aware of my filter, or rather, my lack of filtration. When I'm in this state, my mum often says that I'm in 'Barcode Mode'. Named after how I see the world in black and white,[7] the term Barcode Mode is reserved for times when there are unexpected words in the gagging area. You may also know this notion by another name, the Freudian Slip. Named after Sigmund Freud's theory of the unconscious mind, the Freudian Slip is a term used in psychoanalysis describing people experiencing an error in speech or memory, when this back-seat part of their brain wants a bit of attention. This can lead them to say things that their conscious mind has been working hard to suppress.

Even though honesty is the best policy, I think sometimes I really do say it best when I say nothing at all. I just wish more people in life would take up this same philosophy. I don't mind saying nothing at all. In my world, there is no such thing as an awkward silence. If anything, these so-called awkward silences just prevent

---

7. And because I used to collect barcodes as a child. I think I'm starting to see why I was bullied...

people from saying things that are *actually* awkward. I've never understood the reason why people feel the need to create mindless insolent noise. (I'm aware of the irony of jibber jabbering about jibber jabber, but it needs to be jibber jabbered about.)

I know it sounds harsh, but I don't really care about your best friend's brother-in-law's aunty. What relevance does she actually have to my life? I'm never going to meet the woman. Unless she has a cat that she no longer wants, don't bother bringing her up. Besides, I wouldn't trust a woman who would be trying to get rid of her cat.

I suppose I just prefer 'big talk' to small talk. I can happily talk for hours to someone about anxiety, depression, or suicide, but chatting about the weather? No chance. Unfortunately, wanting to discuss the big issues of the world (instead of flailing over celebrity gossip, like my peers) was yet another social difference that made me stand out like a canary in a coalmine.

I used to ration my mum on how many questions she could ask me in the car on the way home from school. Three was the maximum, and sub queries derived from the main question were also counted in the question allowance. (We introduced this double-tiered system as a later amendment.)

'Did anything interesting happen at school today?' would usually be the first one. In order to answer this, you first have to define the meaning of the word 'interesting'. For me, it's an adjective used to describe engaging or exciting events that grab one's attention or curiosity. Other people's definition of this word always has and will puzzle me. To this day I still can't comprehend that the public lost interest in space flight after six successful moon missions, yet there have been over 82 series of the TV show *Countdown*...

(Typically, I find cosmology, 70's Glam Rock and cats interesting. Unfortunately, my school didn't include cosmology, 70's Glam Rock or cats on the curriculum. In fact, the closest thing I ever got to learning about any of these things was when our English teacher went on maternity leave. It wasn't really the sort of big bang theory I was hoping to learn about.)

The second question would be 'Have you got much homework?' The answer to this would be yes, but I had usually done it all earlier on. I liked to escape the hustle of hormonal teenagers as much as possible, so I spent my lunchtimes doing the activity they hated most, in the place they hated most. Homework. In the library. A place where you actually got told off for talking. What a brilliant idea! Librarians have always been my kind of people. I really don't see why they haven't deployed the Talk Police in other areas of society too.

The third and final question would be 'Did you have a good day?' Much like the first question, you have to define 'good'. This might be exhibiting consistently high levels of certain qualities across a range of activities. For example, in the context of my school day, you could say that the bullying I received was 'good', as it was carried out to an astronomically high standard, and was extremely effective at making me hate my life. I went to a private school, and just like the education, the bullying was also considered premium. I can't deny I got my money's worth.

If you define the word good as something that is pleasant or enjoyable, then no – I did not enjoy the 'good' bullying. But saying I didn't have a good day at school meant that there would be many more than three questions I'd have to answer. I knew that if I was sad, it would make my mum sad. As we have already established, making people sad is something that I try to avoid at all costs.

Masking is a euphemism used by the medical profession to describe what autistic people do daily to hide their traits. But I would describe it more as an emotional straitjacket than a mask. It's not about dressing up and changing your accent for a role. It is a completely Method way of existing. This wasn't about me pretending to be a ghost for a couple of minutes in a hallway. It was about saying goodbye to a tiny piece of myself each time I stepped into the outside world.

As someone who doesn't like attention, I discovered that *compliance was a form of invisibility*. No matter how I was feeling on the inside, as long as I looked calm, collected, and maybe even happy, then no one would know otherwise. You might think that if I can *pretend* to be neurotypical, then surely I can just stop *being* autistic altogether? If you're not sure of the answer to that question, then here are a couple of other questions I made earlier, to help steer you in the right direction:

Would you ask Stevie Wonder to just stop being blind?

Would you ask John F Kennedy to just stop being dead?

I didn't think so. Blindness and deadness have one thing in common with autism. Incurability.

There is no cure for autism. It's not the sort of thing you can pick up on a bus, so the answer doesn't lie within finding a 'fix' for it. The answer lies within creating a better world, with room to recognise every unique and different type of mind. The world needs all types of minds, not just one.

Masking is one of the reasons why girls who are on the autistic spectrum often get a late diagnosis, or sometimes no diagnosis at all – simply because girls tend to have more of an inbuilt awareness that not conforming could leave to negative and noticeable results.

Masking is an incredibly unhealthy mindset; it's not only mentally damaging, but can cause physical damage too.

To some extent, I had been unintentionally masking for most of my life, but when the bullying started, it became a permanent fixture. I realised that the more I showed who I really was and what I was passionate about, the more I was laughed at. But at the same time, I didn't want to be a sheep who liked the same music and tv shows as everyone else. If you get to know me, you'll know that I cannot pretend to like something when I don't, because of my filter. I can't help showing that I love watching the snooker. Or that I prefer to listen to Billy Joel than Billie Eilish. When every trait of your personality gets picked apart on a daily basis, what are you supposed to do? Lie? I thought that was something we *weren't* supposed to do?

I thought I could sort it all out on my own, without needing to get my mum involved. After all, surely that's why schools have a pastoral care department? She had a lot on her plate, so it was the least I could do to ease her load – which is why I masked it from her. If only I hadn't underestimated just how much scaffolding actually went into holding up a smile.

Before being bullied, I didn't feel like I could trust any grown-ups, as I had been let down by them before. My dad walked out on me when I needed him most. My mum was the only person that *hadn't* let me down. I wasn't going to reward her for this by making her sad. That didn't seem logical to me.

When I did get the courage to ask for help, I went to my teachers. Most of them said that bullying was 'character building'. (Apparently, it's just what teenagers do.) Actually, there's no building involved.

Bullying is character demolition, and that is why bullying *doesn't* make you stronger. Maybe from the outside you appear more robust, having been able to survive complete destruction. But that isn't what strength feels like. That's numbness. On the inside, you only feel weaker and more detached from the structure that once held you together. It's only character building when you start healing, mending all those broken pieces – which is a painful but important process that many people ignore.

I thought that by masking how the bullying was affecting me, it would disappear. We're told that mental health is 'all in the mind'; it was only when I started self-harming that I saw the connection between mental and physical health.

Daily bullying became such a normal part of my routine that I interpreted my teacher's dismissal of the situation as evidence that unnecessary pain was an acceptable part of life. No one seemed to mind if other people were hurting me, so I didn't think it would make any difference if I started hurting myself. It just meant that for once, *I* was control of my pain, not anybody else.

But apparently, when you start using your arm as a chopping board, it attracts rather a lot of attention. Unwanted attention. I couldn't see what all the fuss was about. I couldn't tell the difference between the pain I caused to myself and the pain caused to me by being bullied. My peers caused me much more harm than I could ever cause to myself. The wounds on my arms would heal in a few weeks, but the wounds on my soul would take years to scab over, if they ever did.

I couldn't understand why it was fine for others to cause me pain, but it wasn't fine for me to inflict it upon myself. At the end of the day, it was my choice. Being bullied wasn't. But unlike bullying, I realised that if I could control myself in feeling pain, I could also control myself to move on from feeling pain, and to start healing.

It got me thinking. No one can ever see the true effects of what's really going on inside your head. This is why masking is so dangerous; you cannot see the real damage until it is too late. It turned out that masking wasn't as invisible as I thought, as the effort of trying to keep myself together on the inside is what eventually tore me apart: baring my wounds for all to see. The physical effects of masking for all these years had already begun to take over inside my body, and I had absolutely no idea.

But I shan't reveal the full extent my trauma just yet... You'll have to wait quite a few chapters for that. (And I know you will, because humanity relishes a slice of nail-biting drama. Over a third of all television shows contain some form of grotesque crime or murder. It's quite scary when you think about it. All those people sitting next to each other on worryingly wipeable faux-leather sofas, secretly plotting when they are going to deploy the bleach and plastic sheeting. I think my grandparents are in on it. No wonder they are so neurotic about how much space there is in the freezer.)

I just wish there was some kind of Google Translate equivalent that could interpret my first language (Autism) into English. I would be able to express my emotions truthfully without the fear of upsetting people, whether I'm telling them their new hair colour doesn't suit them, or that I need help dealing with a painful personal problem.

It's thanks to the technology upon which Steve Jobs and Bill Gates built their empire, that many autistic people are now able to communicate the help and support they need more easily. Sometimes it's easier to send a text explaining how we feel than it is to talk to someone face to face – even if they are sitting next to you. It can be hard to admit to others how you are feeling, especially when you are struggling to admit those feelings to yourself.

Socialising is also just *exhausting*. If you're like me and you need to spend at least a week in solitary confinement to recover from waving to a neighbour, that's okay. Socialise on your terms, with people that feel safe. If you want to try broadening your social circle, I recommend starting with people that either your family or friends know. The chances are that if your friend is like-minded, then they will know other like-minded people, and (probably) won't be mingling with murder-obsessed pensioners. It's not about quantity either, and a high friend-count shouldn't dictate how 'social' you feel. Sometimes, less really is more, and I'd much rather have just a handful of people that I can rely on than hundreds of ghosts that don't know the real me.

My phone is a tool that I now rely on every day, as I find it easier to say how I feel when I think the only person taking any notice is Siri. Although the iPhone wasn't the first smartphone to be invented, at the time of its creation it was miles ahead of its competition, and launched the mobile revolution.

In the year that Steve Jobs' life was coming to an end, Apple elaborated upon his creation, and introduced features like Facetime, bastardising his face-*less anti*-social form of socialisation. It would be interesting to know just how much control Steve Jobs had over this decision. You can always guarantee that neurotypicals will pervert perfectly autistic-friendly communication.

Unfortunately for me, I was born before the iPhone. I was even born before the infamous Nokia 3310.[8] So basically, I had to talk. Or not. In fact, for the first few years of my life, I was completely non-verbal – from an early age, I subconsciously discovered that there were lots of ways you can communicate without having to speak...

---

8. If you don't know what a Nokia 3310 is, it was the sort of phone that when you dropped it, the phone would break the floor, rather than the other way around.

Born to be Mild

Ostinato

My alphabet is made from a piano's keys
Each note a different letter
They form my words when played together

My vocal chords are made from piano strings
Hammers strike them, like a bitten lip,
As I wonder what to think

My voice is made from a piano's sounds
Reverberating through the air
Nearby hearts fill with despair

My emotions are made from a piano's stillness
As those around me stare and witness
That noise is a weapon
But silence deafens

Charlotte R Faulconbridge

Playlist for Chapter 3

Hello Earth, Kate Bush

Panic Station, Muse

Brown Eyed Girl, Van Morrison

Home At Last, Steely Dan

Born To Be Wild, Steppenwolf

No Spoken Word, Stevie Nicks

The Way It Is, Bruce Hornsby & The Range

Sir Duke, Stevie Wonder

A Whiter Shade of Pale, Procol Harum

My birth was rather traumatic. Almost three weeks past my due date, it was clear I didn't fancy going outside. I was perfectly happy in the warm, dark cave that I'd been used to for nine months. I liked what they'd done with the place. But then, my lease was up, and someone thought it was a good idea to bring in the bailiffs and have me relocated. The trouble was, it wasn't going to be to another warm, dark cave – but somewhere that was the complete opposite.

When people reminisce over their earliest memory, they usually recall the first time they lost one of their baby teeth, their first day at nursery, or their first holiday. My earliest memory was really quite a bit before any of that... the first thing I remember experiencing in this world was none other than the day I entered it.

I wasn't prepared for the shock I was about to receive. Before being brought into every-thingness, all that I had been used to was nothingness. Everything had been dark, in every meaning of the word. A complete void and lack of sensation. Try and imagine what nothingness looks, sounds, and feels like. It is an impossible state to fathom, in the same way that we cannot comprehend infinity. Which is perfectly okay, as the fact you can't imagine these states shows you that you understand them. Even recalling my memories of nothingness seem so unnatural and strange to me. But in the beginning there really was nothing – albeit nothing with a lot of potential.

I had heard many sounds, mostly indistinct murmurs. But there was one sound in particular that I shall always remember. A duet, played by two hearts. That sound was my only constant. What had felt like a different lifetime in itself began to change, as I perceived that nothingness was coming to an end.

Just a few weeks before my birth, I started to sense that something was wrong. What was once calm had become chaos. I was unable to settle or be still. It later turned out that I was breech and the doctors had no idea. And they continued to have no idea, until my mum was in labour.

Despite this complication, the midwife reassured my mum that she'd delivered breech babies before, and that there was no reason to panic. (It's just a shame that someone couldn't have told *me* not to panic, as that was exactly what I did.)

In less than an hour, the decision to perform a caesarean section was made. I say decision – there actually wasn't any deciding involved, as the doctors made it clear it was the only option left. The hospital went into overdrive as the emergency crash team were summoned. Nurses and surgeons appeared out of nowhere and wheeled my mum in the direction of the operating theatre. My heart rate had fallen to 15 beats per minute, and I was being starved of oxygen. I had no idea that what was about to happen would become my first memory of this world – a memory I like to refer to as my first panic attack.

I remember seeing the complete opposite to anything I had been used to. There was no warning or reason, it just happened. When you hear people recounting near-death experiences, they describe having an eerie feeling, like their soul is leaving their body. I'm still not sure if what I was experiencing was my resuscitation, but I have never felt anything remotely like it since.

I hadn't even opened my eyes yet, but I found myself blinded. I felt cold for the first time, and I lost all ability to hear anything, perhaps due to pure shock. That duet I had been so lovingly comforted by was rendered mute. Still being consumed by light from every angle, I felt weightless. I could sense that I was being moved, in this ocean of light, but I had no idea how it was happening.

I knew I wasn't curled up anymore, and I felt completely out of control. Abrupt shock seemed to silence my panic, and I was still. Then slowly, one by one, my senses started to reawaken. I would lose one sense, only to gain another. My stillness was replaced by the freedom to move. Darkness was replaced by light, and the light was replaced by life. What was once a duet played by two hearts became two separate melodies. I was able to breathe again.

My eyes fluttered in time with the bleep emitting from my vital-signs machine. Open, then shut. Shut, and then open. I was greeted by a figure, the figure that had illuminated my nothingness. My angel: in the form of an olive-skinned, brown-haired man, dressed head to toe in blue polycotton, whom I would still recognise if I saw him today. It was his hands that had led me out of the dark. My body settled into his palms, and I felt his fingers cradle my head, his thumb stroking my brow.

Looking at my hands now, I can't even begin to imagine how I once lay in someone else's, let alone remember it like it was yesterday. I stared up at his big brown eyes that would later mirror mine. Even though my blue angel was wearing a surgical face mask, I could tell he was smiling. The creases that concertinaed at the corners of his mask could have only been made by such an expression. He was my first glimpse of the every-thingness that I very nearly didn't have. I was home, at last.

It is quite common for autistic people who have had traumatic births to remember them. When you experience any trauma at a young age, your brain remembers these events, due to an evolutionary trait to try and protect you from the same thing happening again. When our ancestors were still running around in caves, they had only spears and loincloths to save themselves from the dangers of the outside world. So, when a threat did appear, it was important for them to make a note of it.[1]

Luckily, you can't be born twice; but this doesn't mean to say that the anxieties I have today didn't originate from this event. It could be why I find going to new places so difficult, why I have a fear of change, and why I find bright lights physically painful to look at.

You may be wondering why I've bothered to go into the details of my first memory, but I firmly believe that my birth played a huge part in why I didn't speak for the first few years of my life. Not only didn't I speak – I didn't make a single sound. I didn't babble. I didn't scream. I didn't cry. It was like my brain was totally disconnected from my mouth.

---

1. By taking a note of it, I mean grabbing the tail of a wildcat and using whatever bodily fluids you had lying around to paint a mural, reminding your family that bears are not to be messed with.

Making sounds wasn't something that I needed to do to communicate, as when I was just a few months old, I instinctively started to create my own sign language. It never even crossed my mind that I needed to learn to talk. As I got older, people started to question whether or not I was deaf, as all my peers were much more advanced in the sound department than me. It was obvious that I could hear though, as I would always respond to what was being said to me. I just responded in my own way.

All that my mum had to go on was her experience with raising my older brother. He started to talk when he was 11 months old. I was three before I even thought about saying my first word. My brother and I have always been at opposite ends of the spectrum from each other. We are different in just about every way possible. My brother is severely **not** autistic, and he has all the symptoms that go with it. He has always been confident, a bit of a boundary pusher, and a complete cacophony of noise and disruption. Noise seems to follow him everywhere, even now he's a fully grown adult. To put it bluntly, he never shuts up.

Then you have me. I was born to be mild, *not* wild. I have always been quiet, well behaved, and compliant. If anything, my mum was unnerved by such impeccable behaviour – but you can't exactly go to the doctors and say, 'Doctor, doctor, my child is too good!' No one has ever gone to the GP to get a diagnosis for a child who is angelic.

I never had to be told off for anything. Well, almost never. I was told off exactly twice. Once for stealing the chocolate out of my brother's advent calendar, and the second time involved my cack-handed fingers and a brand-new swanky television remote. I could cope with the chocolate thing; I was only upset because I was caught, but the remote-control incident still sends shivers of perturbed grief down my spine whenever it's mentioned, so I just cannot divulge any more details on that one. Still, twice isn't bad in 23 years.

By the time I was three-years-old, my mum knew that I should have been talking – but she also knew that I wasn't frustrated by my inability to speak. She has always accepted me no matter what, and in the same way she accepted my brother's tomfoolery, she also accepted my stillness. She has always loved and treated us equally for who we are, without question.

Almost 90 per cent of human language is made up of facial expressions, hand gesticulations and body movements. My family would speak to me, and I would respond using my own signs and gesticulations. We all understood each other perfectly – we just didn't use the conventional method. They knew I would talk when I was ready.

Unbeknownst to me at the time, it wasn't 'normal' for a child of three to be mute. If I had a pound for every time someone said that something I did wasn't 'normal', I wouldn't have to claim disability benefits, and I wouldn't ever need to think about getting a job. (This would be useful – but actually I'm desperate to work, as I'd like to be independent and contribute to society. I used to feel incredibly guilty about claiming benefits, but then I realised that if society was more inclusive, I wouldn't have to. It's not my fault that I am unable to work. At the time of writing this book, only 14 per cent of autistic adults in the UK are in full time employment. That is the lowest number in employment for any disability. In light of that figure, this book had better do well...)

My mum kept putting off my check-up with my health visitor, as she knew they would flag the fact I wasn't talking. She was worried that they'd diagnose me with a learning disability. She wasn't bothered if I *had* a learning disability, but at that time, a diagnosis meant that I would be side-lined from education, and the doors of opportunity open to my peers would suddenly shut for me. In the 90's, there was (and still is) a massive stigma that surrounded autism, and all other disabilities too. At that time, if you had a label

66   TOO HIGH TO FUNCTION

of any kind, you were condemned to disproportionately reduced education and employment opportunities for the rest of your life.

Luckily, my health visitor was understanding, and knew that the one-size-fits-all system doesn't always work. She gave me an extra six months to start talking, and if I was still mute, more action would be taken. This was when my mum started actively encouraging me to speak. She tried all sorts of techniques, but nothing worked. As it turns out, there was a very good reason for this – and it had a lot to do with the shape of my head.

Ever since I was born, people had been casually mentioning that they thought my head was a bit, well... funny looking. Some time after the appointment with my health visitor, my mum visited a chiropractor, for treatment for herself. My head must have been on her mind, as out of the blue, she asked his opinion. He said that it was so obviously weird looking, he was surprised my mum even had to ask. He advised that she should take me to see an osteopath, and promptly scrawled down a phone number. Willing to give anything a try, she made an appointment.

Osteopathy is an art, not a science. It focuses on the bigger picture, and is a more holistic approach to healing. A treatment that may work for one person may not necessarily work for someone else.

For someone who didn't fit into the one-size-fits-all system, it was exactly what I needed.

We discovered that the reason why my head was a weird shape was because when I was breech, I was resting in a position that put far too much pressure on my frontal lobes. This caused them to come out of alignment, and to protrude slightly. The frontal lobes are located where you might expect, right at the front of your skull, and they are a vital part of the brain. They are responsible for our understanding of consequences, other people's emotions, and speech function. One area in particular, called Broca's area, is a region that helps put our thoughts into words. Damage to this area can hinder the ability to speak and understand language.

It makes perfect sense why I didn't speak, as this part of my brain obviously wasn't functioning properly. My osteopath was able to ease certain restrictions in my body which were limiting my nervous system's ability to develop. Part of my treatment was to have my frontal lobes manipulated into their proper alignment. The day after I had my first treatment, miraculously, I started to talk. It was like someone had flicked a switch and turned on my voice.

I continued to have treatment for around eight months and the sessions kept improving my development. By the time my next appointment with the health visitor came around, my speech was no longer under observation. No further action was needed, so I didn't get referred for a diagnosis of any kind. I'm certain that my life would have been entirely different if I had been diagnosed with a learning disability at this time – although whether this would have been for better or for worse, I'll never know. I'm still not sure whether finding my voice was a blessing or a curse; I think if I was still mute today, I would probably be able to communicate my needs more easily. I still struggle to talk about my emotions. Some of the content in this book will be brand new information for my family and friends, because I never properly knew how to verbalise it before.

I have always been a girl of very few words, and even though I had found my voice, I still tried to find other ways to communicate that didn't involve talking. Some were more successful than others. I remember watching the film *Matilda* as a child, fascinated by the way she moved things just by looking at them. I thought I'd give it a try – but instead of moving objects, I would try and transfer my thoughts telepathically, by staring at whomever I wanted to speak to. It may be no surprise that this didn't work, and just made me look like a psychotic child from an 80's horror movie.

So *that* alternative method of communication was a failure... but I didn't have to look for other options for long – when I started school, I discovered a new language that became my native tongue. Music. In my very first lesson, I was taught the difference between sounds that were major and sounds that were minor. Major sounds were bright and sharp; minor sounds were dull and harsh. My teacher said that in order to tell them apart, music that sounded happy was considered major, and music that sounded sadder was minor. My ears pricked up.

I suddenly remembered how strongly music could grip onto your emotions. I was just two years old when I first experienced this, at a parent and toddler music group. I'd never before seen so many people en masse, all connecting over one thing. If anything, I found it a bit overwhelming, and I was relieved when the other children needed a break. (Although actually, I think they just wanted to find out whether their instruments tasted as good as they sounded. When you're two years old, going from playing a tambourine to eating one is a perfectly logical progression.) What I learned from my time at this Stevie Nicks convention was that the connection between music and emotions was all I needed to marry my thoughts.

A wise man once told me that in order to be a great communicator, you must first learn to listen. It may not surprise you to learn that this wise man was a musician. Music will always be one of the best forms of communication, because it is universal – it doesn't matter what language you use, music speaks to your emotions, not your words.

Music communicates in a way that no human language ever could. It teases feelings out of your soul that you didn't even know existed. You know the kind: that make you admire, desire, forget and regret. It can make you feel happiness as if all you'd ever known was hell. And sometimes, music can deeply wound you. It can creep up on you and strike, inflicting pain when you need to be reminded of what you have, and what you have lost. It knows exactly how to make you listen.

Music makes me feel empowered, but also vulnerable. When sharing my music, it's like I'm putting my heart into the hands of the listener, not knowing if it will be embraced or trampled upon. I'm able to vocalise my thoughts in much greater detail whilst sitting at my piano, but also, I find that I'm much more susceptible to rejection.

There aren't many things in this world that make me feel as deeply as music does. A hug doesn't comfort me, and no kiss has ever taken my breath away. When we don't find immediate pleasure in human relationships, our souls may be left feeling cold. We begin to wonder what it will take to spark that fire in the way that everyone else's seems already to be lit; the way love can defrost the most frozen of hearts. I've come to realise that it doesn't matter how I get that feeling. What matters is that I feel it at all.

My alphabet is made from my piano's keys; each note is a different letter. When played together, these notes form my words. The piano's strings are my vocal cords, and the hammers that strike them are my lips. Being autistic can feel like living in a black and white world – and even though the keys on a piano are black and white, they make me see the world in a million colours.

The beauty of language is that it can always be translated. Whenever I play, I am always understood.

The Quantum Cheshire Cat

I've often seen a cat without a grin, but a grin without a cat! It's the most curious thing I have ever saw in all my life!

Lewis Carroll, Alice's Adventures in Wonderland

Playlist for Chapter 4

Vincent, Don McLean

Mona Lisas And Mad Hatters, Elton John

She's A Rainbow, The Rolling Stones

The Stranger, Billy Joel

Every Little Thing She Does Is Magic, The Police

Drowning Man, U2

Schrodinger's Cat, Tears For Fears

'It's vanilla soup,' I exclaimed. The neurotypicals laughed. I wasn't sure why – that's basically what custard boils down to.[1] But even though I didn't know why they found what I said so amusing, I supposed it's better to make people laugh than to make them cry. Except when you make someone laugh so much that they actually start crying... which is *immensely* confusing for someone who struggles to interpret human emotions.

Emotions: perhaps one of the biggest areas of my autism that still utterly bewilders me. People think that us autistics don't have them. Well, we absolutely *do*; just as much as you. We just don't always know what to do with them, how to show them, or how to recognise them.

I was once described as being emotionally artistic. 'Wow', I thought, 'someone really understands my new and revolutionary thoughts on life's greatest wonders. They must think that my words are like bright strokes of colour being delicately brushed across a blank canvas'. It wasn't until I spent more time with this person that I came to the disappointing conclusion that either I misheard, or they misspoke. They meant emotionally *autistic*... It appears my thoughts were less da Vinci, more Jackson Pollock.

---

1. Although you should never boil custard.

Clashing splatters against a brick wall, chucked straight from the paint tin in a whirlwind of gay abandon.

You might think that making a comparison between our emotions and art is a load of Jackson Bollocks, but for me they share a common factor in our understanding of them: context.

In artistic terms, I am emotionally colour-blind. You can show me a picture of somebody crying and I can easily mistake them as laughing, and vice versa.[2] This is because, without the context, my brain doesn't know what's going on. And the same applies to art. If someone was to slaughter, bisect and preserve a calf in formaldehyde in their front room, people might say they were behaving oddly. But if they happen to be Damien Hirst, they'd win a Turner prize. Context is the key.

Take for example Leonardo da Vinci's masterpiece, the *Mona Lisa*. One of art's greatest mysteries is whether she is smiling or frowning. People look at that painting in the flesh, from multiple different angles, and come up with a different response. This has as much to do with art as it has to do with the way we perceive facial expressions. The way that the curvature of her mouth is painted is

---

2. Bizarrely enough, when I'm crying, I often look like I'm laughing.

a source of ambiguity, because depending on the angle from which we observe her, it can affect the emotion our brains recognise. Especially if we don't have any context behind the painting.

Is she pleased that she was chosen as da Vinci's model? Is she seductively eyeing him up as he bends over to pick up a dropped brush? Is she regretting that prawn sandwich she had for lunch? I guess we'll never know.

My interpretation of Mona Lisa: I think her smile is forced. I'd definitely be feeling a bit fed up if I was told to sit perfectly still for hours on end whilst being painted in various shades of brown. There's no surprise where she got her nickname either; I would have moaned too.

My colour palette is more limited than a neurotypical person's: I'm happy or sad. Angry or calm. I'll either love something, or I'll absolutely hate it. My world is made from superlatives. My emotions are either On or Off, and it can take just seconds for that switch to be flicked. Autistic people tend to have a limited emotional range, so we can go from feeling elated to severely depressed in a matter of seconds. This makes our environment very black and white, and finding the 'shadow-light' in between is difficult. Our base emotions feel incredibly intense most of the time, but it is possible to find the grey area.

People generally imagine that emotions are invisible. They're called feelings because they are things that we *feel*, not see, right? Whilst that may be the case some of the time, understanding the physical connection between our emotions and our bodies is what has enabled me to unlock many more emotions within my range than I could first experience.

Everyone has some sort of physical response to their emotions. Some responses might be more extreme than others, and some might be so mild that we probably don't even think about them. If you don't struggle with identifying how you're feeling, then you might not have noticed this at all. It is, after all, an automated part of being human. But whilst it may seem entirely obvious to most, if you're autistic, this connection between physical and emotional response could be your best chance to distinguish those less obvious emotions.

As well as our hormones producing emotional responses, our emotions can also cause hormonal reactions. Therefore, our emotions can also control how our hormones are produced. Serotonin is the key hormone that stabilises mood, and it impacts our whole body in the process. Not only does it affect our brain by making us feel happier, but the majority of this hormone is found in the gut. Have you ever had that 'butterflies in your tummy' sensation? That's because when we're anxious, the serotonin in our blood causes a shortage of oxygen in our stomach. This translates into that feeling of nausea, to get us to pay attention to the fact we may be in a situation that is causing us distress. Serotonin is also found in our central nervous system, so any dips in this hormone can easily cause headaches, fatigue and muscle tension. So instead of trusting my mind – which isn't always a reliable source – I have found that being able to understand my emotions through my body's physical responses has made things a lot clearer.

As well as my body's behaviour helping to identify my own emotions, body behaviour has helped me identify other people's, too. This is because people don't always tell their faces how they're feeling. It was William Shakespeare (probably) who said that the eyes are the windows to the soul, but this only works if people clean their windows. Often, I sense something completely different within someone than the emotion that's showing on their face. For me, this is where the 'autistic gaze' comes into play (affectionately known as 'the death stare').

I find eye contact an incredibly intense experience, so I try to avoid it. But when I do make eye contact, I can find it hard to break. People have told me that I looked like I was going to punch them, when in fact all I was doing was getting distracted by their inner emotions. When you don't find social interactions intuitive, you're constantly trying to look for clues on how people are feeling, so you can gauge the social context. I find it hard to distinguish if the fluctuations in people's emotions are down to something that I have said or done, or if they are linked to things going on in someone's personal life that have nothing to do with me. I can't tell what it is that I'm intended to see and what is supposed to be hidden. This can make my 'gaze' even more intense, as I'm trying to figure out whether or not *I'm* the problem.

Another reason behind the death stare is a condition known as prosopagnosia. Prosopagnosia is a thirteen-letter word, which when played in Scrabble is a guaranteed triple word score. It is also a neurological condition in its own right, characterised by the inability to recognise or differentiate faces. It is commonly known as 'face blindness'.

A lot of autistic people struggle to recognise faces, whether it is the face of a family member or a complete stranger. Others, like myself, find it difficult to recognise people's faces when they change something drastic about their appearance. For example, every time my brother shaves off his beard, I have to relearn his face, as my brain no longer recognises him. The same goes for if a friend decides to dye their hair without warning, or if we meet up and they're wearing a hat or sunglasses. So, often, the death stare can be my alarming response to these changes in people's appearance.

It's not always easy to outright ask if someone is feeling okay, either. Asking someone how they're feeling and finding out it's something personal is like being caught rummaging around in their medicine cabinet or underwear drawer – so I tend to just stick to asking people that I'm close to. Yes, looking like a serial killer does bother me sometimes, but it's an integral part of how I interact, so not always avoidable. I don't think being approachable always matters anyway. The Queen barely smiled for decades, and no one seemed to mind.

I'm extremely sensitive, so I can pick up on very slight changes in people's behaviours. There is a word for people who are as sensitive to people's emotions as I am – we're called empaths. Derived from the word empathy, we have the ability to understand the feelings of others from outside our own perspectives.

The word *emotion* comes from the word *motion* – because our emotions are constantly moving and changing. People usually have lots on their minds at any one time, like remembering to pick their kids up from swimming and what they need to buy for dinner on the way home. These thoughts can be the small differences between the way someone smiles and greets you, and how quickly their face collapses when they don't think you're looking. Most people are unable to completely conceal these slight changes. This is why I find it really hard to talk to someone over the phone, as I don't have a visual prompt. You can't see someone's body language over a phone call, so I feel even more vulnerable to slipping up in conversation.

People's truths often get in my way. I can tell when someone has just had a spat with their spouse, a laugh with a loved one, or even a death in the family. I can tell whenever my mum has a strict work deadline to meet, as she has very distinct 'tells'. She does well to hide them, as she knows her tension will cause me anxiety, but I can pick up on the slightest changes in her stress levels.

Another trait of being an empath is that everyone else's emotions affect me as deeply as my own. Sometimes, even deeper. If I walk into a room and sense that someone has just suffered a loss, I know that I won't be able to cope with being around that person for very long. As much as I wish to support them, I find myself being overwhelmed by their emotions, and it can take days for me to recover. Autistic people will know that having a high level of sensitivity of any kind is exhausting, but I feel so lucky that I am an empath. Without it, I don't think I'd have a clue about people's emotions at all. Empathy is why I find emotions so magical, because it proves that emotions don't even have to be our own to have power.

Cast your mind back to the first time you ever saw a magic trick. I want you to remember the exact feeling of awe that you felt, as your whole world seemed to turn upside down. Then, I want you to remember the disappointment you felt when you realised it was all a trick: just a big mirror or a particularly bendy lady.

But magic doesn't have to be an illusion. It doesn't even have to be a trick. We all have real magic inside of us, right this very moment. To understand this magic, we have to take a trip down the rabbit hole. Specifically, Alice's rabbit hole – back to the start of the 20th century.

Back then, if you chose to study physics, you were considered as mad as a hatter. (And if you wanted to please your parents, you became an engineer instead.) This is because the wizardry that physicists came up with at this time changed the world as we knew it: quantum mechanics.

In the realms of quantum physics, a particle's state of superposition can be questioned, meaning that a single particle can occupy multiple locations at the same time. Quantum physics is so crazy and twisted that scientists even had to start naming aspects of it after the characters from *Alice in Wonderland*.

The Cheshire Cat was famous for being able to disappear and leave its smile behind: a fictional idea that became reality. In recent years, scientists have been able to separate a particle from its physical properties. They have been able to tear apart a neutron from its magnetic moment, otherwise known as its spin, just like separating a cat from its grin. In doing so, they have plunged mankind ever deeper into questioning the possibilities that surround us. The idea that these particles could exist without their properties – and even stranger, that these properties could exist without their particles – really does make for a curiouser and curiouser world.

This is all very lovely of course, but so far, it's all been happening in a lab. Just maybe, that the same idea of splitting up something physical (like taking apart a neutron from its spin, or putting something into a state of superposition) is possible in our day-to-day lives. In fact, I *know* it's possible, because we do it all the time.

Remember when I told you to recall the awe you felt as a child when you witnessed magic for the very first time? Well, hopefully you did. Hopefully, you managed to remember the very exact trick that you saw. By recalling how you felt, you didn't physically travel back in time to relive the experience as if you were a child again. You simply remembered how it felt to be there, watching a crazed misogynist sawing a woman in half.

By remembering the event and recalling the emotion you felt years later, you are effectively splitting up the properties of the exact moment you saw that magic trick. The moment is physically in the past, but the emotion has been separated. You leave behind the cat, but not the smile. And what if we tumbled further down the rabbit hole? I know this sounds like a bunch of pseudo spoon-bending-nonsense that would frazzle the follicles of an effervescent boffin, but it is the *real* magic of emotions. They can defy the physical state of the world as we know it.

In science, there is no reason why the joy of a friend getting married or starting a family should make us feel good. Yes, it *may* release some serotonin and cause us to feel happy for our friend – but in theory, it *shouldn't*. In fact, we would be a far superior species if we didn't care so much about other people!

Our own particles aren't experiencing the moment, or getting married, or having a child, so why do we feel something? How do we experience the properties of the event, without even living it? Why do we feel the force of the spin from somebody else's neutrons? Physically, it doesn't make any sense, and at the moment, there is no explanation as to why we do this. It's incredible how the human mind can separate the physical matter of a moment from its energy in this way. We take the power of our emotions for granted. Empathy is pure magic, because it allows us to escape the prison of our own experiences and journey into the life of another human. It's the reason why reminiscing over old memories can make us laugh, cry, and fall in love all over again.

The human brain is one of the most complex things in the known universe.

(I know. Terrifying! I'm sure we have all had moments when we've done something and thought: 'that was definitely *not* the behaviour of the most complex thing in the universe'. But despite this, our brains are constantly sneaking around, doing things we don't even know about.)

In the same way that we can feel happy for someone when we, ourselves, have not experienced the happy-making event, we can also experience responses to events that haven't even happened yet. This is the dark side to superposition. As someone who has suffered from anxiety for most of her life, I am no stranger to the power that fear can have on the mind. The area in the brain that stimulates our fight or flight response is called the amygdala. The amygdala is necessary for survival, as it triggers our body into a state of high alertness, so that we will be aware of any immediate danger. This state of high alert can be exhausting; it can often spring up on us suddenly, and cause very real and physical symptoms – but this is a necessary response. Otherwise, its design would be completely useless.

Imagine you are swimming in the ocean, and you feel something brush past your leg. Perhaps it's a piece of seaweed, or a harmless fish. But what if it is a shark? You have no idea whether there is a threat nearby or not. This is the exact moment when our brain doesn't have time to reason with us anymore; as it begins to plot our escape from the potential lurking danger, it plays us a little announcement:

```
'You are possibly swimming in shark-infested
waters. Remember, when one is potentially
swimming in shark-infested waters, one should
swim a lot faster.'
```

The problem is, our brain delivers this helpful update in a slightly cack-handed way. Instead of sounding like a calm public information film from the 1970's, it turns this message into a psychological thriller, in which we are getting mauled to death by a Great White. This is how panic attacks are brought on, because our brain can't decipher the level of threat we're experiencing. We don't regularly find ourselves about to be swallowed up by a megalodon,[3] but we may feel the same level of anxiety towards something that is ordinarily mundane, because that response has been forever planted in our DNA.

This is the brain's remarkable response – the response that protects us from harm every single day, without us even knowing it. For a feature that has ruined many otherwise picturesque moments of mine, I still have to admire its quite impressive design. If you have experienced anxiety, then you will know how debilitating it really is, and how we can become suddenly paralysed by our own thoughts.

To me, having a panic attack feels like swimming in an ocean, knowing exactly how to swim, yet finding myself drowning – and the worst part is, I never actually die.

Our bodies sometimes misinterpret the physical symptoms of anxiety, mistaking them as being a threat to our physical health. A tight chest can make us feel like we're suffocating, a raging heartbeat can make us feel like we're going to have a heart attack. The key thing to remember about panic attacks is that the

---

3. I hope.

anxiety can't *actually* hurt us. Yes, it feels excruciatingly painful, but in reality, only a real-life threat, such as an actual shark, can truly cause harm. That doesn't mean we should try and get rid of this response altogether, as it helps us escape from *actual* life-threatening situations. We just need to help ourselves understand the process better.

When we're anxious about something that is *actually* happening, our brain is just doing what it was designed to do. But when we have irrational, anxious thoughts about things that are imaginary, our brain stops being rooted in the present. The remarkable thing about that is, because the amygdala still triggers that emotional response, we still get all the physical symptoms of anxiety as well. This is an example of how our brains have become too powerful for our own good. I like to explain this is by using physicist Erwin Schrödinger's famous thought experiment: Schrödinger's cat.

A cat is placed in a steel box along with a vial of poison, a hammer, a radioactive substance, and a Geiger counter. When the radioactive substance decays, the Geiger counter triggers the hammer to release the poison, which subsequently kills the cat. But there is no way to determine when, or even if the radioactive substance will decay. Until we open the box, we will have no idea whether the cat is dead or alive, because the fate of the cat is tied to whether or not that substance decays. Schrödinger stated that the cat must be *both* dead and alive until the box has been opened – because without opening it, the state of the cat is completely unknown. So, we have to consider that the cat is *both dead and alive* at the exact same time.

(I do just want to clarify that Schrödinger never actually put any cats in boxes. He only chose the cat to show just how uncomfortable he was with this idea of uncertainty, so arguably this makes him more of a cat curator than a cat terminator.)

The whole idea sounds benignly bonkers, as I never open boxes to find cats that are both dead and alive at the same time. Understandably, the theory led to arguments spanning decades, with people fighting over whether it's the person who opens the box that decides if the cat is dead or alive. Does the cat decide for itself? What if you stick Schrödinger in the box and see how he likes it? Some might ask why he even bothered putting a lid on the box at all.

But if we think outside the box for a minute, and feel Schrödinger's fear by applying this logic to anxiety, it validates the reason why we feel anxious over events that haven't happened yet. My mum recently had a biopsy, and whilst waiting for her results, I observed that we both lived in this state of unknowingness so perfectly described by Schrödinger. We imagined what life would be like if her results were both clear and not clear. It was only when we opened the box that we knew what was inside.[4]

My mind always jumps to the worst possible outcome, so I spent most of my energy imagining the worst-case scenario. Imagining the implications of this nightmarish reality was just exhausting, and I lost my ability to enjoy the present moment. A term that I like to use for this train of thought is 'disaster-movie-thinking'.

Disaster-movie-thinking describes the chain reaction of frenzied thoughts that we experience when we constantly imagine the worst-case scenario. All rationale spirals out of control, and we're left laboriously coming up with the next plot twist in the disaster movie that is our life. If you think about all the disaster movies you know, they have one thing in common. They are all unrealistic. When I realised this, I learnt something very powerful about my anxiety: I will never be able to stop awful things happening. I will never have control over whether the cat is dead or alive. Life will be full of both live and dead cats – but why waste time and energy ruining all of the good moments by catastrophising about everything that could go wrong? Understanding the difference between *how our brain wants us to feel* and *the reality of our situation* is fundamental in beginning to overcome anxiety.

---

4. In this case, it was actually an envelope.

Despite the rampant animal cruelty, what Schrödinger managed to create was a theory that not only helped us understand the foundations of the universe, but also how to live in our own little worlds too. You may have heard of the term 'mindfulness'. Despite its millennial connotations, mindfulness does not involve hiking in Tibet or clanging tiny cymbals together whilst sipping green tea. (Sure, you can if you want to, but it's definitely not mandatory.) Mindfulness is based on a set of practices that help ground us and make us more aware of the present moment. Its core practice is to tune into our senses and become more aware of our surroundings. Contrary to popular beliefs, it is not a distraction technique. It is actually the complete opposite. It encourages us to stop imagining the fate of the cat, and to just open the box of our senses, so we can focus on the things that are real.

It's not about sitting perfectly still and turning ourselves into living statues either, as even all the active types out there can incorporate mindfulness into their lives. I personally like having a mindful cleaning out of the fridge, going for a mindful scrub of the bathroom sink, and mindfully changing my cat's litter box. Find a real cat, preferably one that's alive, and keep living in the present.

Even though anxiety is something I wish I didn't have to deal with, it reminds me to live more fully in the moment. It shows me that

I really do care about the wellbeing of others – perhaps a little too much – and it's also a useful tool that has helped me change many aspects of my life. Anxiety is never a particularly fun thing to feel, but I use it as my motivator when I need to make a positive change. It is an excellent arse-kicker when you need it most. Ultimately, only *you* can control what you think, so only *you* can control how you feel.

All of the good, the bad, and the truly ugly parts of our minds prove the very magic and power of human emotion; why we feel happy for other people, and get anxious over imagined events, even when the laws of physics state that it's impossible. Tricks and illusions lose their lustre the moment we understand how they're done, but I think our emotions only ever get more magical.

The Protrusion Presumption

I've had a lot of worries in my life, most of which never happened.

Mark Twain

Playlist for Chapter 5

(Don't Fear) The Reaper, Blue Öyster Cult

Baba O'Riley, The Who

Confusion, Electric Light Orchestra

Tricycle, R.E.M.

People Are Strange, The Doors

Diamonds on the Soles of Her Shoes, Paul Simon

Walk Of Life, Dire Straits

Laughing on the Outside, Bernadette Carroll

'If you forget your protractor, you'll die.' That was what my primary school maths teacher told me one Monday morning, and it made quite a lot of sense to me at the time.

You see, if you don't remember to bring your protractor to your maths lesson, then you can't complete your trigonometry questions in class and you won't pass your maths exam. If you can't pass your exams, then you won't get any qualifications. If you have no qualifications, then you can't get a job, and without a job you will have no money. Without money you can't buy food, and without food you will inevitably reach a painful, malnourished demise – slowly starving to death.

I know what you're thinking. Why couldn't I possibly have asked the person sitting next to me if I could borrow *their* protractor? Well, the same teacher who had warned me about missing-protractor-death also told me that if I spoke in class, Death would follow me, haunting me night and day, awaiting my acceptance...

My teacher clambered onto his swivel chair, spinning theatrically. 'Time will pass, and Death will grow, as she makes more and more friends. One day Charlotte, you will see Death. She will try to chase you down, forcing you to run away from her.'

By now he had captivated the rest of the class in the throes of laughter. His chair had gained enough momentum that he was able to reach out a hand to decapitate the poor skeleton stood next to his desk, with whose skull he started to passionately converse, articulating its jaw in my direction.

'You will reach out to Death and tell her your story. The story of the time you, Charlotte Robyn Faulconbridge, asked Lyle Sargent if you could borrow his angle measurer. In that very moment, even Death will shed a tear for the pain of Life; for the way it had treated you.'

Stunned into dazed confusion, I began to ponder my options. Both apparently led to dying. So, I opted for the one that provoked less anxiety, and made sure to always carry a protractor wherever I went. It didn't ever occur to me over the two years of dramatic antics performed by this hyperbolic, theatre-going-luvvie (interspersed with an occasional bout of improper fractions) that my teacher might have been joking.

Taking things literally is a common complication in the way autistic people communicate. It's not that we lack understanding of the words you're saying to us – we just have a different way of processing the information we're receiving.

Language has two layers of meaning. There's what we *superficially* mean (being the literal definition), and what we *really* mean (the figurative definition). This is where the phrase 'figure of speech' comes from. It's easy to tell the difference if you're neurotypical, but if you're autistic, you can often get the wrong end of the stick.

We like facts. You can't interoperate them. They just mean what they state. This, in tandem with our sometimes-obsessive natures, is why you'll find that autistic people are often walking encyclopaedias in their favourite subjects.

Dyslexic people will always ask, 'Why can't words just be spelled how they sound?', while autistic people ask, 'Why can't people just say what they mean?' This is one of the biggest barriers I face in communication, but with a little practice and patience, I have started to understand what people are truly saying.

I used to think that taking things literally meant I was stupid and unimaginative, but I now know it's just down to the autistic filing system. Our brains sort everything out as completely separate pieces of information, so connecting them altogether is an additional step. An optional step, in most cases! Unless something is completely spelled out to us, we won't see it.

A few years back, I was given the email address of a professional that I had been told could help with my anxiety:

therapist@happylife.co.uk

The *rapist*? At happy life?? I was horrified. Why would giving me the email address of a sexual predator help my anxiety? It had completely the opposite effect, obviously. After the initial confusion and shock, I found myself conflicted, in particular, by the use of the word 'happy'. It seemed a bit problematic that this person was blatantly advertising how the effects of sexual misconduct made them feel. At least they were being honest – plus, being upfront about a crime does tend to lessen your sentence. I couldn't decide if they were being incredibly smart or incredibly stupid.

When my mum asked me if I had sent this person an email yet, I was bewildered. She was in favour of this? Mum went on to explain to me that she understood how scary starting therapy must feel, and that we would take this step one session at a time. I was even more confused. Therapy?

After a closer glance, I realised that the email address was, in truth, simply the contact information for a therapist – a very good therapist, in fact. This is just one of the many examples of how my brain can mislead me with information. Hitler's another one.

...I should probably explain what I mean, before I start bandying around the names of fascist dictators in such a confident manner.

Autistic children often get confused between what is real and what is not, especially when it comes to films and tv shows. We tend to just believe that what we're watching is *the case*; it's sacrosanct. My favourite film as a child was *The Sound of Music*, and for years, I genuinely believed that Hitler was still alive – because my brain struggled to make the connection between the year we live in now and the year the film was set. Yes, I am fully aware of how ridiculous that sounds, but my brain simply couldn't make that distinction. I just grew up thinking that the people of Austria lived in a state of continual fear.

There are some upsides to this. One of them is that Auties are great at doing what we're told – if we're told step-by-step and in great detail. When people ask me what day it is, I'll say it's Sunday the 2nd of April 2023. But apparently, most people aren't bothered about knowing the month or year; they're only interested in the day itself. Hey, I'm only trying to give you the full conversational nine yards that is so often insisted upon; you neurotypicals better make your minds up.

Here is a typical conversation in my house, when I'm asked to assist with cooking the dinner:

Mum: *Did you tell Charlotte to put the dinner in the oven?*

Gran: *Yes.*

Mum: *Did you mention anything about actually turning the oven on?*

Gran: *Ahh...*

Often, these misunderstandings cause great hilarity – like the time I was talking to a friend who happened to mention that he knew someone who was a space manager. A space manager! I couldn't understand why he hadn't told me about him sooner. My friend *knew* that I had always loved space. He blabbered on about how the two of them met, when all I really wanted to know was *which area of space was he supposed to be managing?* Which space station did he call home? Which one of the many star meadows did he look out on as his back garden? I hadn't even been aware that space managers existed... So many questions!

I hadn't been aware they existed because, as it turns out, they don't. Well, they do exist, but they are more commonly known as room allocation coordinators. That was ten minutes of my life that I'll never get back.

This literal part of my brain is also responsible for why I don't always understand when sarcasm is being used – and believe me, it gives me and my friends a lot to laugh about. But there was one time when it really wasn't. The year before I was diagnosed, one perfectly innocent sentence turned my life upside down.

It wasn't a cold, damp or stormy night. It should've been, due to the shenanigans and frolicsomeness that lay ahead, but that's the weather for you. You could describe the fallacy as being rather pathetic. Or you could say that the weather was merely trying to make me feel calm, by putting on a display of tranquillity. Whatever the weather's reasoning, it wouldn't have made any difference to the raging anxiety that had already begun to simmer inside me.

A lump. On my knee. The size of a golf ball that's been sliced in half, or one of Kermit the Frog's eyes. I'm no medical expert, but I don't think that a lump the size of a golf ball that's been sliced in half or one of Kermit the Frog's eyes was ever considered to be a good thing to find on one's knee. Needless to say, my sleep the previous night had been non-existent.

After weeks of physical examinations, x-rays and scans, that day we finally received the news that it was nothing sinister or dangerous and the lump needed no further treatment. I was still confused as to why there was a lump on my knee in the first place, and my mum, in all her loveliness, did what any parent would do when her child was tense with trepidation. She tried to reassure me that there was *definitely* nothing to worry about.

(Two words come to mind that sum up the so-called light-hearted reassurance that followed: the first being 'big', and the second, 'mistake'. Sometimes, when recalling the events that took over the following nine months of my life, a third and final word can be inserted. It's a verb that rhymes with ducking, and it is best placed before the start of the phrase or plonked slap bang in the middle of it.)

We had just raced back through the rain to the car from my final doctor's appointment. My mum turned and saw my exhausted, confused face gloomily staring back at her. She swept my soggy fringe over to one side and said, 'You don't need to look so worried anymore – the doctor said it's only a small bone spur. Your body obviously decided to just grow a third leg.' She smiled and proceeded to start the car, turn on the radio, and began the drive home, as if nothing had happened. As if everything was perfectly ordinary. As if she hadn't just informed me that I was, in fact, growing an extra limb.

Just growing a third leg? There was no 'just' about it! I was profoundly speechless. This was far worse than anything I had researched online.[1] I didn't say anything, because I didn't want to know. If only I *had* said something... Oh hindsight. What a barrel of ducking laughs.

I still couldn't understand why mum had said it so casually, as if it wasn't ever going to be a problem. Getting shoes to fit, was my first thought. I have always found shoe shopping utterly horrendous. Thanks to my genetics, I am blessed with feet that resemble two slices of pizza. Not cheesy, but narrow at the back and considerably wider at the front, like two slightly deformed triangles. They're not even the same length – my left foot is bigger than my right by a whole shoe size. Also, I would have to get specially made trousers, as I wouldn't be able to fit my extra leg into my current two-legged kecks. I noted that it was a good job my mum had studied fashion and textiles at college.

Then my mind went back to the basics. For instance, the simple factor of how I would walk. I would have to re-learn that for a start. Maybe I would move in a similar way to a spider, carefully articulating every one of my joints in a precise sequence. Or

---

1. I probably should have been able to foresee that typing 'third legs' into Google was going to give me slightly more explicit search results than I would've hoped for. If there had been a cesspit nearby, my phone would have belonged at the bottom.

perhaps I'd end up bumbling round like a Reliant Robin with a slightly wobbly front wheel. The latter is more my style.

I tried really hard to think of the positives that a third leg would bring to my life. Could be ideal for some types of exotic dancing? In the future, when people commented that I danced like I have two left feet, they would actually be right. Having an extra limb would be a great talking point in social situations. I find it easier if I can come up with a few prompts to help me steer a conversation in the right direction when talking to someone new, or at a large social gathering. This might even deter people that I didn't like that much from talking to me altogether. Huzzah!

I began to think more strategically. I imagined that this kind of phenomena could end up making me and my family a pretty penny or two. People would pay to see me and my adverse appendage. 'The Human Tricycle! Coming to a village fete near you!' Even though I despise unnecessary attention, I would do it for the greater good. Then I began thinking about the darker side to fame and fortune... Would it change me? For better or for worse? Send me down a path of remorse and regret? Yes, yes – of course there are all the perks of a lavish celebrity lifestyle (the sex, drugs, and Rosalind from the parish council's homemade sausage rolls), but I was worried about the effect that my newfound stardom might have on my family. One phone call from a persuasive grad student with too much time on their hands, and I'd be found comatose on a slab being used for medical experiments, in exchange for a holiday in the Caribbean. All in all, it was a tumultuous time of great uncertainty.

A couple of days passed, and the initial shock had begun to wear off. I realised that my disaster-movie-thinking wasn't helping – I needed to think more short-term, and take each day as it came. I didn't know how long it would be until my life was changed forever.

The doctor said that if the lump grew, I would need to let somebody know. I could only assume that they meant I needed to be keeping an eye out for the arrival of a few toes peeking out behind my kneecap. I couldn't keep this a secret from my friends any longer. I was going to have to tell them.

Bizarrely, they didn't seem shocked. At all. Why was no one freaking out about this except me?? What was wrong with them? If I thought my mum acting casually was strange, I certainly wasn't expecting the same reaction from everyone else. Even the Reverend at school didn't bat an eyelid. In fact, all the advice and support he gave me was to get myself on the council housing list as soon as possible, claim benefits, and live my life as an eremitic monk. I wasn't going to complain about the lacklustre responses to my bizarre physiological future though – I dislike attention – but you have to admit, it was rather odd. I supposed there was freakier shit going on in the Bible.[2]

At this point, I decided that I should just be grateful for my family and friends. I was going to trust everyone's else's calmness, and I went from panicking about never being able to wear high heels again to thanking all those around me for making me feel loved. I resolved that the idea of having three legs would grow on me, like a patch of mould on a bathroom ceiling. Everything was going to be okay: all my worry about me changing – for better or for worse – was unnecessary. I wasn't going to change, because no one else had.

Nine long months crept by, and there was still no sign of another leg. Not even an ankle. I wasn't entirely sure what the incubation

---

2. Like when David the Supplanter delivered two hundred Philistinian foreskins to his future father-in-law as the dowry for Princess Michal. I guess with all that in your lap, a third leg pales into insignificance.

period was for extra appendages, but to put it frankly, it was starting to take the piss. I'd have had better luck waiting for Godot.

You can do a hell of a lot of things in nine months. Like growing an actual whole human for example, with two legs. I was only waiting for one. I decided that I would bring the topic up at my next doctor's appointment. The appointment was completely unrelated to the lump on my knee; it was the start of my autism diagnosis process in 2015.[3]

We'd gone through all the usual rigmarole of explaining my traits and how they affected me, and after a substantially lengthy discussion, I thought that now would be the perfect time to ask about the impending arrival of my additional limb. The room fell silent. The doctor glanced over at my mum and smiled awkwardly, whilst awaiting some kind of reasonable explanation as to why I would possibly ask such a question.

My mum looked over at me, her expression as confused as the doctor's. Could she have forgotten about it? I guess nine months was a long time, but *surely* she would have remembered this? She glanced back at the doctor, then back to me. This went on for

---

3. I was officially diagnosed on Friday 13th November later that same year. Hilarious, right?!

quite some time, as if she was recreating some kind of Chuckle Brothers sketch with her eyes. I couldn't believe I was going to have to remind her.

I reminded her.

There was a sudden eruption of laughter. It continued. For quite some time. Not seeing the humour of the situation, I abruptly asked why they were both making fools of themselves.

My mum had rewound back to nine months earlier, the day we were both sitting in the car whilst the rain pattered upon the windscreen, and realised my mistake. Apparently, what she said was just a joke to try and make me feel better.

Just a joke?!

Just a joke.

I was confused. It didn't sound like a joke to me. A joke is supposed to be a play on words. A witticism. A passing quip, a thigh-slapper, a comic juxtaposition of opposing ideas to provoke an instantaneous explosion of laughter.

This couldn't had been a joke, because I didn't laugh.

As the two of them continued to smirk through to the appointment's conclusion, I felt ever more stupid. Cunningly, I already looked stupid, so that particular joke was on them.

I was furious.[4]

Whether my mum's erroneous comment qualified as a joke at the time, who can say – but I can laugh about it now. Mainly because I understand a lot more about why I took what my mum said so literally. I also understand that if there's ever a time when I'm not sure if someone is joking or not, I can just ask them straight away, just to be sure. As for my friend's responses back then, they

---

4. I was almost as cross as my mum on the day she found out that women didn't really have one more rib than men because of God using one of Adam's to create Eve. She was outraged that the Bible had lied to her, because God wasn't supposed to lie to us like that. She argues that ancient civilisations were just a lot more advanced in stem cell research than we had originally thought. (No reservations over the immaculate conception though. That was all tickety-boo.) She was 36 when she had these revelations. For all those people who are still unsure as to whether autism is a genetic condition or not, what more evidence do you need?

probably thought I was just joking too; dry humour tends to be more natural for autistics.

Looking back on that day, sitting in the doctor's surgery, I can't help but feel like I should have led with the question about my third leg, instead of us spending hours agonising over whether or not I had an autism diagnosis. I think I might have saved everybody a lot of time and energy...

Casino Rationale

Remember to look up at the stars and not down at your feet. Try to make sense of what you see and wonder about what makes the universe exist. Be curious, and however difficult life may seem, there is always something you can do and succeed at.

Stephen Hawkins

Playlist for Chapter 6

Disorder, Joy Division

Change, T. Rex

Castles Made Of Sand, Jimi Hendrix

You Know My Name (Casino Royale Soundtrack), Chris Cornell

Live And Let Die, Wings

Cars, Gary Numan

Nobody Does It Better, Carly Simon

Road to Nowhere, Talking Heads

Rebel Rebel, David Bowie

The Universe is more disordered now than when you started reading this book. If I made a cup of tea and then left it, it would go cold. Ever wondered why? The answer is the same for why weeds overtake gardens, why ancient ruins crumble, and why cars begin to rust. It all has to do with entropy.

Entropy is a measure of disorder. There are far more *disorderly* variations in our lives than *orderly* ones. Imagine that you've just tipped over a box of jigsaw puzzle pieces. In theory, it is possible for all of the pieces to fall perfectly into place to create a completed puzzle. But in reality, this never happens – quite simply, because the odds and variables are overwhelmingly against it. There is only one possible state in which the pieces would fall in perfect order to create the finished jigsaw, but there are almost an infinite number of ways for them to fall in a state of disorder.

Autistic people are creatures of habit. We like structure, order, and individually we are about as flexible as an iron statue of the pope. The reason why order is so important in our lives is because it helps us to understand a world that makes no sense to us whatsoever. Order is the calm amongst the chaos, the method in the madness, the joy within the jumble in all of life's uncertainties. In a world that doesn't make sense to us, we try and seize control over every aspect we can.

Most people can get up, get washed, dressed, eat breakfast, and go about their day without another thought, as if they are permanently set on autopilot. Perhaps one day, you get called into work earlier, which in turn means that there is only time for a shower, not a bath. Because you have to leave the house earlier, you will have toast for breakfast instead of cereal because you're out of milk, and your online grocery delivery won't arrive until an hour later. If you're autistic, then this slight change in routine will be enough to create a chain reaction of disruption that will impact on the entire rest of the day, and possibly many days after.

Change is life's only constant. It is a concept that we never quite get used to, and it is an autistic person's worst enemy. Entropy only ever increases over time, but there is some good news: you *can* fight back against the relentless pull of this force. You can solve a jumbled-up puzzle. You can eradicate the weeds from your garden. In order to combat my fear of the ever-evolving Earth, I live my life by rigid routines that help keep me grounded. The only thing I ever really enjoyed about school was that there was a weekly timetable that I could follow. I knew exactly what was going to happen, and when. The worst time of year for me was the summer holidays. Whenever they were approaching, I felt like I was about to jump off a precipice, because there was no structure to that large expanse of free time.

There are parts of my daily routine that may seem utterly pointless and irrational to someone who is neurotypical. For instance, I have to keep my door open at exactly the right angle, and everything in my room has to be in exactly the right place. I even have to eat the food on my plate in size order, starting from smallest to largest. If, for any reason, something or someone stops me from completing these rituals, I get incredibly irate and a meltdown is inevitable. Those techniques – when I feel like I am briefly taking control of my environment – are how I feel comfortable in the world.

There is great debate in whether these regimented routines and behaviours are healthy or not, and whilst I do agree with both sides of the argument, we first have to figure out where the traits come from. Mild cases of autism are commonly misdiagnosed as obsessive-compulsive disorder (OCD). You can, of course, be autistic *and* have OCD, as I am, but the majorly overlooked factor within telling them apart is the difference in motivation behind the behaviour.

OCD is a condition where someone is driven to complete certain routines, shrouded with the fear of something bad happening. You might have suffered a traumatic event, which leads to you latching onto certain patterns of behaviour that you feel compelled to do, to make sure that the event never repeats itself. However, the ritualistic behaviours of someone on the autistic spectrum show that we don't complete our behaviours out of fear, but because they make us feel good. I often feel ashamed of my OCD behaviours as they are a lot more irrational, and as a logical person I am aware that they don't make any sense. However, my autistic routines make me feel happy and calm, as they are my positive coping mechanism.

With OCD, I am consciously doing these behaviours, and the fact that I feel compelled to carry out the rituals makes me feel incredibly anxious. The feelings of anxiety are temporarily relieved once the rituals have been performed, but they soon return again, causing the cycle to repeat. A lot of the time, people with autism aren't aware that they are completing their routines, because it feels like such a natural thing to do. Because the nature of the motives behind each condition are contrasting, they must be handled differently.

As we have already established, autism is a lifelong condition, so trying to banish certain traits is just not feasible. Our routines are what help us function as best we can, so you'll find that stripping those away will only make things worse. But – there is a balance we have to achieve. Encourage the routines that support your brain function, and slowly discourage the routines that stop you functioning altogether.

When I was younger, I was once barred from my local corner shop for rearranging the shelves. They thought I was trying to shoplift, but all I wanted to do was to make sure that the labels on all the items were facing the right way,[1] so they were properly aligned. Although this behaviour made me feel good, it's an example of an autistic routine that, if allowed to get out of hand, would impact me every time I wanted go to the shops.

It took a long time to work out some kind of solution, as I used to have to re-position objects in shops and at friends' houses on every visit. The solution I've found that worked for me was to restrict these behaviours to certain places – specifically, my own house, as doing those behaviours at home isn't going to impact other people.

Putting this into practice has allowed me to restrict all of my stimulating behaviour[2] to my own private spaces, so that I don't upset people when I'm out and about. I can go out to see friends or go to the shops, knowing that when I come home, I can line up all my pens and arrange my bookshelf in alphabetical order, then

---

1. Well, my way.

2. You may have heard these of actions (such as rearranging objects or fiddling with things) described by another name, stimming – derived from the word 'stimulating'.

by colour, then by genre, then back to alphabetical, as many times as I like.

The obsession for order doesn't stop there. When autistic people want to know something, we aren't satisfied with just knowing a little bit. We have to know why. It comes as no surprise, when you realise that some of the most pioneering minds throughout history have been autistic, that this is a common trait. We tend to fixate on a handful of niche subjects, and when the inquisitive part of our brain makes friends with the obsessive part, wonderful things can happen.

After being inspired by my older brother, I decided one day that I was going to teach myself to play the guitar. I could already play the piano and the drums, so why not become a one-woman band? My motivation behind pretty all of my music is that it releases stress, so only good could come from it. I have to admit though, as far as stress toys go, a guitar is quite an expensive one. With my obsessive nature partnered with my desire for knowledge, I went from playing *Jack and Jill went Up the Hill* to Jimi Hendrix in a matter of weeks.

When autistic people decide to do something, whether that's learning an instrument or memorising the entire map of the London underground, we don't stop until we've *done* it. I should also add that we won't stop until its perfect. I have the precision of a first-class marksman, so anything less than perfection won't do. At heart, this virtue is a positive one, but I have suffered for the price of perfection many times.

I was once so determined to learn a particular piece of music that I actually gave myself a cyst on my hand. I had to rest my hand for six weeks whilst it healed – which meant I lost the use of my most valuable asset, both for me and my anxiety.

Just like my routines, my obsessions come from a place of keeping myself calm, relieving stress and feeling safe. My first obsession was no exception. This fixation began at the age of six: unable to sleep, I tip-toed my way down the stairs and peered through the crack in the doorway to the living room. 'The name's Pond, James Pond.'

I sat and watched, as Mr Pond was frantically trying to escape the clutches of a bald man who owned a very distressed looking cat. Pond didn't stand a chance, as he didn't have a cat – and we all know that cats rule the world. The bald man probably had an entire army of angry, fluffy killing machines, just ready to pounce and claw the face off whomsoever he desired. It wasn't a fair fight.

Then Pond pulled out a gun, and brought a new meaning of 'fair fight' to the table. After a clattering of gunshots, a few thrown fists, and remarkably no harmed cats, Pond leapt out of a nearby window and commando-rolled around a corner, where his ticket to safety was waiting for him in the form of a car.

But this wasn't just any car. It was far different to anything I'd ever seen on the roads before, and definitely in a different league to my mum's Renault Megane. Eagerly awaiting Pond's arrival, it sparkled under the halo of a flickering streetlamp. It was sophisticated, striking – yet its edges were as soft as the bald man's head (and his cat). Its eyes took the form of perfectly round headlamps, and it wore smile of one reuniting with an old companion: friendly, and full of teeth. Emblazoned on the front of its silver chest, positioned right over its heart, lay a pair of wings. The wings that would fly Mr Pond to safety.

Pond flung open the door, slid into the driver's seat and ignited the fire in the machine's eyes. Its dormant heart had abruptly awoken and begun to pound – and it kept on pounding, until Pond was out of the clutches of the bald man and his furry assailant. Luckily for Pond, his guardian angel had thoughtfully left his name placed between the feathers of his wings, so Pond would know who to thank. The name was Martin, Aston Martin.

I was shaken.[3]

Everything about Aston was beautiful. I had to know more. From that moment on, I became his most persistent stalker, and I spent weeks finding out everything I could about him. Top Gear was flowing out of my telly on tap, and for years I spent my weekends religiously visiting motor shows and car museums. My mum would suggest that we should do something different for a change. You know, spice things up a bit? But I never got bored of seeing the same cars, week after week. The more I went, the more I enjoyed going, as those cars became familiar territory. Knowing that every Sunday I had a predictable environment was exactly what I needed before the next lot of chaos ensued.[4]

I always looked forward to seeing what car Pond would be driving next. And I didn't just look forward to seeing *what* he was driving, but *how* he was driving it. Whether he was twisting through the air, deep sea-diving, or skating across a frozen lake, these cars seemed to do absolutely everything. I was particularly impressed when one of Aston's friends seemed to vanish with the push of a button. What better way to hide and to escape from bald men with cats than to

---

3. Not stirred.

4. Otherwise known as Monday morning.

own a car that could turn completely invisible! For someone who doesn't like attention and who actively tries to be as unnoticeable as possible, I decided that this was the one for me.

The first time I ever saw an Aston Martin in real life was at the seventh birthday party of one of my classmates. It was at a soft play centre. Not exactly my idea of fun – but come to think of it, I'm not sure that spending your Saturday afternoon in a large, hot, overcrowded shed full of screaming children oozing a whole variety of bodily fluids[5] was really *anyone's* idea of fun. But apparently, when you're seven, you haven't really known 'fun' unless you have experienced a full attack of the senses.

The reason I had to attend this all-too-realistic Hell-on-Earth simulation was because somehow, the loud and obnoxious spawn of Satan whose party it was had attended *my* birthday celebrations, and social etiquette dictated that it was polite to attend his. I'm not fully up to date on the societal protocol of seven-year-olds, but I'm pretty sure that inviting your friends to hang out in an old warehouse decorated with snot, spit and sweat was definitely *not* polite. I woke up one morning to find my party dress hanging on the back of the door. That sequin-encrusted vision filled me with terror. It was party time. Again.

---

5. Some of which are yet to be identified by scientists.

In an attempt to mask my authentic autistic self – in the hope of fitting in and making friends – I allowed myself to be driven to the party like a lamb to the slaughter. On arrival, I was horrified. Giant red letters, burning themselves onto my retinas, spelled out 'Jimbo's Jungle Jym'. I knew that these soft play centres were designed purely to separate the predators from the prey. Very much a *live and let die* type scenario. They were a modern reconstruction of the evolutionary Darwinian concept: only the herd's fittest survive. A form of natural selection, such as a pride of lions working together to chase down a herd of zebras or antelopes – the difference being that *these* lions could use a swinging rope to catapult themselves into the herd, knocking them off their hooves and into the bottom of a ball pit, left for dead and never seen again.

If you were lucky enough, these predators would occasionally chuck a trainer at your head, and you could lie there, hoping that the shoe would imbed itself so deeply into your skull that you would completely forget about the events that had taken place. I knew I wouldn't make it out alive. I wasn't a zebra. I wasn't even an antelope. I was a blade of grass growing on the African shrubland that the antelopes and zebras ate for breakfast.

I desperately needed something to happen so that I wouldn't have to spend an afternoon with demonically possessed children, and it needed to happen fast. My time was running out. I had barely even walked halfway across the car park when I saw it. My beacon of salvation outshone those giant red letters of doom. It was Aston.

I couldn't believe it. He had come to save me, just as he had saved Pond. I sped over to where he was waiting, and studied his every feature. I was fixated: it really was *him* in the flesh! Even though my mum seemed to have a rather different understanding of seven-year-old social etiquette than me, we both agreed that this wasn't an everyday event. I'd choose being culturally captivated in a car park over getting mauled in a mosh pit any day. I'd be seeing the lions and the rest of the herd[6] at school in less than 48 hours, for five consecutive days, for far too many weeks of the year. Statistically speaking, this was a one-day-in-seven-years event. There was no point in trying to drag me away.

Shortly after I began to fawn over Aston, a figure wearing an AM branded T-shirt started to approach me. He had to be a fellow admirer. But it soon became clear that this wasn't just a fan – he had not only bought the T-shirt, but the car to match. Before he

---

6. All that was left of them.

had a chance to introduce himself,[7] around roughly half a million questions bubbled to the surface of my brain.

I started asking Mr Nice-but-Clueless everything I could ever dream of knowing about Aston, ranging from how many transmissions the gearbox had, to what hue of crimson the brake lights glowed. But the more questions I asked, the more I seemed to know more about his car than he did. Nice-less was out of his depth.

He didn't seem to appreciate the miniscule details that went into the craftmanship of producing his car at all. It was all utterly wasted on him. It wasn't until I was much older that I realised that the sort of fan who bought this sort of car wasn't interested in the mechanics of what they drove, but more about how it seemed to increase the size of a certain appendage. Poor Aston. He was being used as a form of materialistic Viagra. He deserved better.[8]

I *did* get to sit in the driver's seat though. I was allowed to flick on the ignition so I could hear Aston's voice – I noticed he growled

---

7. Or to warn me about what would happen if I touched his most prized possession.

8. Just a heads-up, chaps, Viagra does not turn you into James Bond. But it will make you Roger Moore.

in the key of A major, perfectly accompanying what was playing on the radio: *Cars* by Gary Numan. Listening to the lyrics, this was a song about a man who would use technology and material objects to distance himself from human contact. He viewed cars as the tanks of modern society, stating that he felt safest of all being locked inside. I instantly knew that Gary must have gone through a similar soft-play-centre crisis. (It wasn't until I became a Glam-Rock-obsessed teenager that I discovered Gary Numan had been diagnosed as autistic. He used music as his escape from the stresses of reality, a sentiment that had only just begun to resonate with me.)

Sitting in the driver's seat, I looked through the windscreen at those giant red letters that had now pleasantly unburned themselves from my soothed eyes. I watched children in various states of woundedness, begin to tumble out of the building, having been reminded of exactly where each stood in the food chain. Just like Gary, I was safe. Safe from the savage hunting ground that is a children's soft play area.

By now, I had asked all the questions I had wanted to ask apart from one – one which, when I put it to Nice-less, seemed to cause much amusement. It turns out that Aston Martins don't *actually* vanish. (And that the surname of the particularly lucky protagonist I'd grown envious of was Bond, *not* Pond.) That feature was apparently a one off, made especially for him. But that didn't matter to me, as my love for Aston went even deeper than I had originally thought. After all, he had just saved my life.

I worked out that in order to buy one of my own, I would need to save up my weekly pocket money for seven hundred and seventy-one years. Not thinking I'd have the patience to wait that long, I decided I should try and focus on being able to acquire just one part of him: the winged badge upon his chest.

I spent many weekends foraging in scrap metal yards, in the hope of being able to get my hands on one. The search was tiresome, especially as it reached the colder months. Rusty, derelict junk heaps turned into diamond mines overnight. When the frost fell, renegade appliances and the carcasses of once-pounding machinery became jewels glistening in the winter sun. I felt like a pirate searching amongst a trove for my treasure... but my treasure was nowhere to be found.

That is, until a few weeks later, when I *did* find it, in my Christmas stocking. Buried right at the bottom were my very own pair of Aston's wings. They were the best present of all that year; in fact, one of the best presents I have ever received. They sparked my interest in other cars too, and in the new year I began treasure hunting all over again. I've hoarded boxes full of hundreds of car badges ever since, but Aston's wings still take pride of place on the window ledge, next to my bed. Whenever I glance over at them, they remind me of the guardian angel I befriended all those years ago.[9]

Right back from the book of Genesis, we have been warned off from feelings of doubt and suspicion. From the moment Adam and Eve were tempted by the snake, the seeds of uncertainty were planted and have blossomed ever since; they now live intertwined with humanity. We have been raised to believe that to feel suspicion is a sin, and that to query the unquestionable is a crime. But without those thoughts, we would never learn anything. We would never be brave enough to question the world, even if we turn out to be wrong.

---

9. Years later, when I was 16, an extremely kind friend of my Occupational Therapist drove me to prom in his Aston Martin. A few months later, he received an invitation to attend a private VIP tour of the AM factory in Gaydon. We had only met once, but he knew how much I adored them, so he invited me along for the ride. It was such a special, grounding experience for me. (Thank you, Mike. I loved every second.)

Stephen Hawking's famous black hole radiation theory turned out to be incorrect, but after thirty years of questioning his work, he solved one of the biggest mysteries in physics. He made a complete U-turn on his original idea. It takes immense courage to admit to being wrong, and even greater courage to prove why.

I think this is why science gives people a sense of anxiety and detachment, as sometimes there just isn't always a reason for why things seemingly go so wrong in our lives; there *isn't* a logical order to the Universe. In fact, science can be truly terrifying.

At the time of writing this book, all of the stars, galaxies and planets that we can see only make up around 4 per cent of the known universe. The other 96 per cent is unknown, made up of dark energy and dark matter that we cannot see, detect, or even fathom. The fear of disorder is more than understandable, but entropy can be beautiful.

There was once a time when there was incredible order. A time when there was nothingness. Then, from that nothingness, we gained everything that we see today. Everything around us is a manifestation of disorder. On the way to that increased disorder, we have been given all the things we find so beautiful. Our galaxy, the stars within it, and all of us, are symptoms of disruption.

For me, the most inspiring example of entropy's consequences are the poppies that bloomed upon the battlefields of Flanders Field after the First World War. The fact that one of today's most recognisable symbols of peace came from overwhelming violence is the true definition of beauty, in its messiest and most poetic form.

Entropy's ever-increasing velocity is frightening, but to understand its beauty, you need to spend some time with it. I used to think I was so unlucky – like the world was punishing me for not being like everybody else. There was a time in my life when everywhere I went seemed to become a battlefield. Chaos followed me. But I've come to realise that without all the tears and the turmoil, I wouldn't be who I am today. Yes, it was chaos, but it was *my* chaos.

The things we autistics obsess over may seem irrational and annoying at times, but in the end, all we want to know is *why*. Why six strings attached to a block of wood makes a sound. Why internal combustion engines power our cars. Why the you-ness of you and the me-ness of me makes us who we are. Curiosity is, without a doubt, one of the greatest forms of rebellion – so go forth and rebel.

The Enigma Variations

The Only One

*It's like I'm the only one who can feel
The Earth spinning on its tilt
Yet no one believes me
As everything looks still*

*It's like I'm the only one who can feel
Our planet hurtling around the sun
Yet no one believes me
As everything carries on*

*It's like I'm the only one who can feel
We're falling through time and space
Yet no one believes me
As nothing ever breaks*

*It's like I'm too alien for Earth
Too human for outer space
Yet no one believes me
As I wear the same old face*

Charlotte R Faulconbridge

Playlist for Chapter 7

Shout Above The Noise, Penetration

Do You Really Want To Hurt Me, Culture Club

The Boy In The Bubble, Paul Simon

It's Oh So Quiet, Björk

Enjoy the Silence, Depeche Mode

Singin' In The Rain, Gene Kelly

Cool Cat, Queen

Mad World, Tears For Fears

Blackbird, The Beatles

Nimrod (From Enigma Variations), Edward Elgar

How many autistic people does it take to change a lightbulb? None; we're just relieved it's broken and we can finally take our shades off now. And if you don't want a detailed monologue on the history of the filament, you'd better do it yourself anyway.

You possibly already know that autism is a neurological processing disorder that affects the brain – but you may not be aware that it also affects the entire nervous system. Sensory processing refers to the way the nervous system receives messages from our bodies and turns them into responses. When we think of our sensory inputs, we think of the sense of sight, smell, hearing, taste, and touch... but there are actually three additional senses that also affect people with sensory processing problems.

The first is called proprioception, which is our ability to move and make mind-to-muscle connections; the second is our vestibular sense, our ability to balance and be spatially aware; and the third is our interoceptive sense, the internal sense that helps us recognise when we are hungry, thirsty, or in pain.

Our senses are the foundations of our fine motor skills, emotional function and self-regulation, so any discrepancies between the brain and the nervous system will have an unruly impact on day-to-day life. Sensory difficulties aren't confined to an autism diagnosis either – our nervous systems can play up for a whole variety of reasons.

A sensory processing disorder means that sensory information is received by the brain, but doesn't get organised into the right place. This leads to an incorrect response to the stimulus. People on the autistic spectrum will experience lots of variation in sensory problems; for example, from being too sensitive to light or sound, to not being able to feel certain sensations at all.

If you have sensory difficulties, then you will most likely fit into one of two groups: the sensory seekers, or the sensory avoiders. Sensory seekers' nervous systems are hyposensitive: under-responsive to a lot of sensory input. Sensory seekers may find that they aren't as aware of other people's personal space, that they can't help but touch and fiddle with objects around them, and that they are somewhat clumsier than others. This is all because they are trying to compensate for a lack of recognition in their nervous system. To help boot up their nerve endings, sensory seekers can find it helpful to participate in more hands-on or messy activities, and make sure they are regularly physically active.

People often misdiagnose sensory-seeking disorders with attention deficit hypersensitivity disorder, commonly known as ADHD, as the characteristics present in a very similar way. In the same way we talked about the differences between OCD and autism, the difference between these two conditions is also to do with the *motivation* behind the behaviour. People with ADHD often find it hard to sit still and concentrate, and the same goes for sensory seekers – but the reason why is completely different.

People with ADHD find their brains will process information slower than others, so need to manually generate the required level of activity for the brain to work more efficiently. By moving and fidgeting, someone with ADHD is instinctively breathing their brain back to life – like winding up a mechanical toy for a longer period of time to make it travel further. Trying to suppress the impulse to move will only make things worse. It seems counter intuitive to everyone else, but if it works best for you: just do it. (Appropriately!)

If you are a sensory seeker, you will experience the same impulse to keep moving – but this is to kick-start your nervous system, not your brain function. Sensory seekers often struggle from a lack of proprioceptive input (sense of movement), so keeping themselves gently moving will help create a better mind-to-muscle connection. Of course, it's possible to have both disorders, but it's important to identify the cause and behaviours of each, so you can implement the correct treatment.

At the opposite end of the scale is where you would find me, with the sensory avoiders. I'm hypersensitive, which means that I am oversensitive to sensory input, and I try to avoid it. In contrast to sensory seekers, sensory avoiders will usually come across as nervous and quiet. Sensory seekers won't be as aware of other people's personal space, but as a sensory avoider, whenever I see another human being, my natural response is to get out of the way. We are very particular about the clothes we wear, the food we eat, and the people we touch, which can make us appear precious and spoilt. But it's really not the case.

If you're a sensory avoider, the slightest change in your natural environment can be overwhelming. I am constantly trying to keep my environment predictable, so I'm not distressed by unwanted sensory inputs. I don't do this because I'm picky and neurotic – I do it because my nervous system interprets unwanted stimuli as *physical pain*. I find bright lights, loud noises and light touch all incredibly painful, because that's how my nervous system interprets this information.

Every time I go to the supermarket, I have to prepare myself mentally and physically. As soon as I get through the doors, I am met with bright Gestapo-interrogation-style lighting, the jarring noises of tills clanging shut, and cold gusts of air wafting from the freezer aisle. All of those different sensory inputs cause me great anxiety because I know that my nervous system won't process the information correctly. And the worst thing is, I can't control any of it – yet more reasons to dread going outside...

There *are* some things I can do to control my environment. I'm able to create a 'mobile bubble', almost void of sensation, that I can deploy when things get too much for me. I have indoor sunglasses with dark blue lenses that counteract harmful artificial light. (I do have outdoor ones as well, but luckily for me, I live in England, where Vitamin D is a delicacy – so the chances of a summer as hot as a shirtless Leonardo DiCaprio eating a chilli pepper whilst posing for a calendar celebrating the history of the electric oven are low.) But it isn't just bright lights that are visually challenging; I can be easily overwhelmed by busy surroundings. If you ask me to find something in a crowded cupboard, the chances are I won't be able to; my brain just can't single out objects when they are all cluttered together, and they turn into one big pile of mess. This is why I always keep my bedroom tidy; being around mess makes me feel restless and clutters up my mind palace.[1]

I also take a pair of earphones with me wherever I go, to block out unwanted noise if necessary. Humans can hear up to around 90 decibels without feeling discomfort, but if you're hypersensitive

---

1. I say mind palace; it's more of a mind shed.

to sound, that threshold drops to around 60 decibels – around the same volume as having a normal conversation with someone. Any sudden noises that are louder than this can cause my ears to start ringing, and I get intense, throbbing headaches that have been known to last for hours. Whenever my brother mows the lawn, it sounds to me like a group of historians are re-enacting the Battle of the Somme in my back garden.

Of all my senses, sensitivity to sound is by far the most painful, simply because of where and how long the effects last for me. As the auditory sense is located in the inner ear, on either side of the human head, I can't switch my brain off to that input. My reaction to unexpected/heightened noise is so intense that it completely takes over, and all I can do is wait until it goes. Sometimes, the pain is so extreme that my body goes into a 'fight or flight' state, as at a deep level, my brain thinks I'm being attacked. In order to try and stop the 'danger' (and bear in mind, the danger appears to be coming from inside my head where my ears are located) I instinctively start attacking myself, to try and get rid of the noise. Banging my head against the wall, tearing at my skin, and even hitting myself are just some of the things I have been known to do when sensory-overloaded.

As well as loud noises, I also find unknown noises distressing. For me, night-time is never quiet. If you listen closely, all those noises that were disguised during the day suddenly take centre stage. Even if they're quieter, the fact that they disturb the stillness is alarming. This is why I had to have someone sleep in the same room as me for many years, as I could never get settled enough to drift off.

I always carry a hairbrush in my bag, so that when I'm anxious I can get someone to stroke me with it. (Sure, other things calm me down too, but it's not always possible to carry a cat or a piano with me...) Yes, it sounds odd – but being brushed, whether it's my hair, arms, or my back, really comforts me. I am tactile-defensive, particularly to light touch, so applying deep pressure to my body really calms down my touch receptors. This is why you'll find me wearing thick jumpers and leather jackets all year round, as light and floaty summery fabrics are enough to cause me discomfort.

Now, I want you to stroke the hairs on your forearm extremely lightly. So lightly that you're barely even touching your skin – you'll probably have a similar sensory response as to how you'd feel when being tickled. Normally, people laugh when they're being tickled. I don't laugh. This kind of sensation on my skin would cause me to cry, scream, and act aggressively until it stopped – my nervous system interprets the sensation of light touch as a blinding pain that feels like I'm being electrocuted.

In the past, I've been known to tear out my own hair, because on days when my nervous system is especially sensitive, even the feeling of my hair lightly touching my face can bring me to a boiling rage. I get anxious when I'm outside and get caught in the rain, as the sensation of raindrops on my skin feels like tiny pin-pricks piercing my flesh: I remember going on a bike ride when I was younger, when it started absolutely hammering it down. We were over an hour away from home, with no car or shelter nearby, and I started screaming because of how intensely painful it felt. I kept on screaming until I was home and dry. I guess I'll never know why Gene Kelly loved singing about it...

Okay, now, I want you to slap yourself. Yep, that's right. Right in the same place on your forearm that you just stroked.

Only joking, you don't really need to slap yourself.[2] If you did, you'd probably say 'ow', because it would hurt. But for me, that would in fact be the *right* pressure of touch for my nervous system. When I ask to be stroked with firm pressure, I'm actually giving my nervous system the input it wants.

---

2. Sorry about that.

Being this sensitive to touch is why I find physical relationships difficult. People often think that autistic people don't have a heart, and we get compared to characters like Spock from *Star Trek*. The language of love is supposedly a foreign dialect to us. But remember, Spock was still half human. It's not that we don't want to show or receive physical affection, but just that we don't always do it in a conventional way. When it comes to touch, not everyone understands the unusual pain threshold for hypersensitive people. It takes me a while to get to a point in a relationship when I can fully trust someone; when I know that they aren't going to hurt me.

Physical relationships aren't the only thing bearing the impact of my tactile defensiveness. I am obsessed with hand washing and hygiene, because if I touch a substance that really shouldn't belong on my hands, the sensation is amplified and upsets my touch receptors. Even if I get just the tiniest speck of dirt from the garden or a splash of milk from my cereal onto my fingertips, I'll probably have a meltdown, and will instantly need to find the nearest wash basin. It makes me feel physically ill when my hands are blemished, as it's as if whatever is on them becomes a part of me. For me, the sensation lingers even after the substance is gone – our skin cells actually have a memory. The stem cells in our skin remembers immune, inflammatory, and stem cell responses, so when we damage our skin, our skin cells know how to heal themselves. Unfortunately for me, my skin's memory is as good as my brain's.[3]

This is why I have such an attachment to my cats – when I find good sensations that sooth my senses, I just can't get enough of them. The world is full of more things that upset my nervous system than make it happy, and it's rare to find something so relaxing.

As well as taking a pair of sunglasses, some earphones, and a hairbrush with me whenever I leave home, I tend to bring my own food too, as I find eating a real challenge. Food has always been the enemy, right from when I was little. This is not because I was conscious about the way I looked, but because the textures and flavours of different foods have always been challenging to my taste buds. Because of this, I tend to eat bland foods. A lot of foods

---

3. I hardly ever eat crisps, as they are a sensory nightmare. They seem to shed and multiply as I get further through a packet, leaving their remnants all over my fingers. Those small scraps of potato shrapnel feel like tiny sharp pins penetrating my skin barrier.

can make me gag, because I can't tolerate the different tastes and textures. I can't even use mint-flavoured toothpaste because the sensation of mint burns my mouth; I use flavourless toothpaste instead.

This response to food actually has a name now: the 'white food' diet. It gets its name from the fact that most foods that are bland or lacking in taste are usually white or pale in colour: bread, pasta, and cheese are just a few examples. This diet is common among autistic children and young adults, as eating plain foods is all that our nervous systems can process. It's not that we choose to be picky eaters, but the sensations caused by different textures, flavours and temperatures are all too much to handle.

For me, this same response ranges across every one of the different food groups. Cabbage is equally challenging for me to eat as caramel.[4] I was seven years old before I had my first sandwich, because until then, the idea of mixing multiple different foods together had been too much to handle. My mum would slice me some bread, grate me some cheese, and chop a knob of butter into my packed lunch, and I would eat them all separately... really, I was just ahead of my time, as if you were to walk into a Michelin starred

---

4. I actually tried caramel for the first time last week, and I cried because of its stickiness.

restaurant and ask for a sandwich in 2023, that's pretty much what they'd give you. Everything's deconstructed nowadays.

Even now, the most complex dish I can cope with is lasagne, and it's taken years for me to finally be able to eat one. I still have to make it exactly the same way each time so that I know all the tastes and textures are perfectly uniform; even the slightest imbalance will make me unable to eat it.

Every other sense is received externally and processed internally. But with food, you have to ingest it before your body can process it. What makes being sensitive to food so difficult is that food is how we get our energy, and how we stay alive. So, when eating turns into a fear, it can be one of the hardest things to overcome, purely because it's such an integral part of being human.

From my personal experience, you should never try and force someone to eat certain foods if they have an eating disorder, as that will only make things worse. Once you make food the enemy, it becomes dangerous, and will only make it harder to conquer. Only try new foods on your terms. Try them with another person if you want. That helped me a lot, as it's always less scary if you can share the experience with someone else. And remember that when trying a new food, it can take up to 20 times to find out whether you actually like it or not. So make sure to persevere!

The biggest thing I have learnt from my eating journey was that food is just a tool, and not the solution to the problem. As I've already mentioned in this book, our hormones play a really important part in our emotional function, and most of our serotonin is made in our gut. When we get anxious, serotonin causes a shortage of oxygen in our blood, which causes our stomach to cramp, ache, and make us feel nauseous – to try and protect us from danger. When we make food the enemy, the mere mention of eating will fill us with dread, which will knock our stomach into a state of fight or flight. How then are we supposed to eat, when we feel sick to the stomach?! It was only once I stopped making food the *focus* and became able to lower my anxiety levels linked to eating that my diet improved – and eventually, I was able to brave eating more challenging foods. The connection between anxiety and the gut is vastly overlooked, but it could be the key to a lot of people's sensory issues around food.

People with sensory difficulties don't necessarily find every sense problematic. There will often be 'rules within the rules'. The best example I can give you of this is to do with my vestibular sense, which controls your sense of balance. Up until the age of fourteen,

I was a competitive figure skater. According to the gospel of Saint Sensory, I should automatically have terrible balancing skills – and in a lot of areas in my life, I do. Just last year, I tripped on the top step of my staircase and broke my foot. Yet I can jump, spin, and dance on the ice as if it were easier than walking.

So having sensory difficulties isn't as black and white as it seems. I find that the calmer I am, the better the chance that I'll be able to cope with exposure to louder noises, brighter lights, and new kinds of foods. Not that I welcome these things into my life with open arms, but the less anxious I am, the less my nervous system wreaks havoc.

For me, hypersensitivity is the most mentally and physically painful part of my autism. I hardly ever show it, but really, I live an extremely angry existence. There is a lot of pain in my world. Sometimes it's caused by extreme events, like the clanging of an alarm bell caused by a fire drill. But most of the time it's just caused by the domestic normalities of everyday life, like hoovering, touching a sticky door handle, or someone calling the dogs in from outside. My life is pretty much spent having meltdowns from being sensory overloaded, recovering from those meltdowns, getting things done for a few days, and then having another meltdown from being overloaded. The cycle is continuous. The truth is, 90 per cent of the time, all my brain is trying to do is to stop me from screaming. Sometimes my sensory issues make me feel completely insane, because I know that no one else around me experiences the world in the same way I do.

It's like I'm the only one who can feel the turn of the Earth; like I can feel us hurtling around the sun, falling through space. We know it's true: we are travelling at an average of 18.5 miles a second, 67,000 mph, 1.6 million miles per day. Yet people don't believe me, as everything is still.

And yet... that is also the one saving grace to this painful condition. Because I'm so sensitive to light and colours, I get to see the world as if through a pair of high-powered binoculars. I'm able to appreciate apparently insignificant beauty in things that others may not even notice. This one of the reasons why I, an adult in her twenties, still get so excited whenever I see a rainbow. You can only begin to imagine how vibrant one looks like to me!

A lot of people only see the night in greyscale: the sky a black wash of dark, the stars pin-pricks of white light. But to me the night sky is anything but monochrome. If you look closely – and I mean *really* closely – then you'll see that the sky is never actually black, and the stars are anything but white. They gently twinkle, dancing through a plethora of hues from blue to red. The bluer a star appears, the hotter and younger it will be. As stars age, they run out of hydrogen to burn, which decreases the amount of energy they emit. So older stars will have a reddish tinge and won't always be as brightly lit in the sky. Those details – that don't tend to matter to a lot of people – really matter to me.

Having a heightened sense of hearing means that my passion for music is always fuelled. I never sit and listen to music to relax. Instead, I like to analyse it. My brain can't help it. From trying to figure out the timing and the instrumentation, to working out the key of whatever I'm listening too, I encounter music as a puzzle to be solved.

A lot of people ask me how I learnt to play by ear. I'm afraid my answer is far from creative: I use mental maths. It's like you've already been given the answer, but you have to work out how to get there. If I want to play the song that I'm currently listening to, I'll sit at my piano and calculate the gaps between each note, like doing one long sum. I split the sum into two parts, one part for the right hand and the other for the left. I then make sure to keep things balanced, as you would when solving an equation, and play those two parts in time with each other, dividing the smaller beats of the right hand into the larger ones of the left. I am able to do this within seconds, whilst I'm listening to the song I want to learn. By the end of the piece, I'll have an accurate idea of how it's supposed to be played.[5]

Beyond my enthusiasm for music, my finely tuned hearing allows me to hear sounds in a much greater detail, almost like I'm the one actually making the sound. Every background noise is amplified, which can be incredibly comforting (depending on the sound!). From the purr of my cats to the call of a blackbird, I can always hear life.[6]

I am also able to hear sounds from miles away. Quite literally in fact, as there are train tracks just over two miles from my house, and I can always hear them when they pass by. There is absolutely no point in trying to whisper around me, as I'll be able to hear you. (Although, other than listening in to people's secret conversations – something that I would never do – I really don't know how ability this could be particularly useful in my everyday life, other than if I wanted to become a spy so I could work for the government...)

---

5. My friends all call me 'The Jukebox' as I can do this on demand.

6. Although there is a particularly screechy blackbird on my patio right now, and I'm starting to question what Paul McCartney ever saw in them.

My hypersensitivity *does* make me feel like I'm part of a secret society, as I can often see and hear things that other people don't notice. It makes the world so much more magical, and I love discovering new and beautiful things about it each day. Talking of secret societies,[7] I was once advised to join MI5 (I was told that because of my enhanced visual and auditory receptors, my skills would be well received). As crazy as it sounds – that the government would recruit autistic people with sensory processing disorders to help save the world – it has actually already happened.

In 1939, a man named Alan Turing took up a full-time role at Bletchley Park in Buckinghamshire, to help crack the secret messaging system that the Germans used to communicate during the Second World War: the Enigma code. He created an electro-mechanical device called the 'bombe', which was able to decipher encrypted messages sent to and from the Germans via Enigma machines.

Around the same time, Austrian and American scientists Hans Asperger and Leo Kanner were (separately) in the throes of

---

7. A thing that apparently, you're not supposed to do.

carrying out research on what was then called 'Asperger's Syndrome'. Because it was such a new condition, it would had been impossible for Turing to have had an ASD diagnosis. It's important to note that you can't simply hurl around a retrospective diagnosis until it fits, without careful research and consideration – but Turing's case has now been studied by experts in the field, who have concluded that he experienced all of the Gillberg criteria for autism in males.[8] He was characterised as having speech and language problems, non-verbal communication difficulties, intense all-absorbing niche interests, and poor fine-motor skills. Reportedly, he was also highly un-reciprocal in social engagements and had many rigid routines, such as having a compulsion to eat an apple before bed without fail. It would seem that he was autistic.

At the same time that Turing was endeavouring to crack the Enigma code, people elsewhere in Europe with his same condition were among the millions being persecuted, by the very regime that Turing's genius helped to bring down. He was lucky to be born on this side of the Channel, and lucky that he didn't have a formal diagnosis – as if he did, he might well have been subjected to

---

8. The Gillberg Diagnostic Criteria was the first criteria used to determine ASD traits, from 1989.

inhumane intervention to try and 'cure' him of the condition, just as he faced immense suffering through attempts to rid him of his homosexuality. Following a year of such authorised 'treatment', Turing commit suicide at the age of 41.

People blamed Turing's death on his sexuality and disability, and yet he helped to end the war. Neither his autism nor his sexual orientation got in the way of that. (And being autistic would only have fuelled his logic and intelligence.) You have to ask the question: did he really commit suicide because he was autistic and homosexual – or because of the way he was treated as a result?

Let's relate that question to the here and now, and my experience of everyday life. If we started designing public places that were dimly lit, had low sound levels, and that were a lot less chaotic – I'd still be autistic, but I wouldn't be disabled by my environment anymore. It's a similar principle to the idea that it's not the wheelchair that makes someone disabled, it's the flight of stairs.

The average life expectancy of someone with autism is 54 years old, and the main cause of death is suicide. I have never felt pushed to the edge by simply being autistic – but I *have* been there due to people's misunderstanding and assumptions about me because of my condition. No one with autism should be made to feel invalid or undeserving of this life for being who they are. The fact that

Alan Turing's astounding contribution to the war effort is not more widely acknowledged will forever remain an enigma to me.

Up the Wooden Hill to Bedlam

Dark is kind in all sorts of ways. Dark hides things –
like shabby furniture and the hole in the carpet.[1]
from The Owl Who Was Afraid of the Dark, by Jill
Tomlinson

---

1. Reprinted by permission of HarperCollins Publishers Ltd ©
(1968) (Jill Tomlinson)

Playlist for Chapter 8

The River of Dreams, Billy Joel

Lullaby, The Cure

Dreams, Fleetwood Mac

Ocean of Night, Editors

And Dream Of Sheep, Kate Bush

We Didn't Start the Fire, Billy Joel

Under Pressure, Queen & David Bowie

The stars bow their heads silently, and the moon yawns as she slips off her shoes when her day is done. For many people with autism, a good night's sleep is an elusive pleasure, and when we wake, we find that our get up and go has gotten up and gone.

Sleep deprivation is harmful for anyone, but if you're autistic, then it can amplify certain difficulties. Sleep isn't just about getting our physical energy; it powers our minds. At the end of each day, we urgently need to reset, as the brain cannot function without this time to recharge. Lack of sleep affects our mood, our ability to make decisions, and our ability to think clearly.

So, what causes disrupted sleep in people with autism? For a start, a lot of autistic traits directly affect sleep. Anxiety, hypersensitivity, and repetitive behaviours will make it difficult to relax enough to be able to doze off. But there is another reason, directly linked to the hard wiring of the autistic brain, that doesn't allow for peaceful sleep.

Melatonin is known as the sleep hormone, as it regulates your body clock and circadian rhythm. The circadian rhythm is our internal time-keeping system; it tells our bodies when they should be sleeping and when they should be awake. Melatonin is produced by the brain in response to different levels of light intensity. Melatonin levels will typically peak around midnight and gradually fall as the sun rises. Levels will remain low all throughout the day, and as soon as night falls, the cycle will begin again.

Melatonin production in autistic people is irregular – no one is one hundred per cent sure why, although there is scientific evidence to suggest that certain genetic mutations could be responsible. Unfortunately, there are no magic solutions for instant sleep. There are definitely some more active approaches, like anaesthetics, or being hit over the head with a cricket bat.[2] But please don't fret. A good night's sleep is never completely off the table, as there are many proven ways that can help train our brains to produce melatonin at the correct time.

Sleep hygiene is an integral part of my bedtime routine. No, I don't mean that I always have a bath before bed...[3] I mean that I have a specific set of positive practices that I use every night, to help settle my mind and body down, so that they are ready for sleep. My bedtime routine usually starts several hours before I want to go to sleep, as it can take a while for the pineal gland, where melatonin is produced, to secrete the desired amount of this hormone.

---

2. Not recommended.

3. Although this can help.

The first step is to make sure that the place I use for rest is a calm environment. You can't fall asleep in the middle of a war zone, so tidy that room up! As we know, autistic people have to actively process every piece of information that their brain receives, so the less we have to process before bed, the easier it is for our brains to start winding down. My room is typically quite minimalist. It is painted in neutral colours; a tidy and ordered environment. If you can't completely de-clutter your space, then make sure that the things that fill it calm your sensory processing responses.

It is also important that we relate the space where we sleep to *sleep*. It sounds obvious, but try and avoid any activity in this space that isn't directly related to rest.[4] If you associate your bed with where you work, read the news, or watch television, it will make it more difficult for you to be restful here when you need to be.

Again, this is kind of stating the obvious, but comfort is probably the most important factor when getting your den ready for roosting. If you're the type of person that can happily fall asleep on the bathroom floor after a night out, then good for you. But I'm the sort of person who would detect that pea under a colossal mound of memory foam. Getting a good night's sleep is one

---

4. Except for, you know – that – as the chemicals released after sex can actually help you feel sleepier.

of those things that will always be worth the investment, so do whatever you need to do to get comfy.

As long as you're not the owl who was afraid of the dark, make sure to block out as much light as you are physically able. Being in darkness instantly tells our brains to increase melatonin production – so this is the most effective way to train that brain for sleep. Whilst on the subject of light, the more sunlight that we're exposed to during the day, the better regulated our melatonin production. There is a direct link between Vitamin D and melatonin; when absorbed into the body, Vitamin D actually becomes a hormone. Melatonin contains the chemical melanin, and melanin is produced in the skin through exposure to the sun. The more sunlight we get during the day, the more melatonin our bodies will be able to produce later on at night.

This, of course, is another factor which impacts sleep for people with autism. Since us auties struggle with being exposed to bright lights, including the sunshine, we correspondingly struggle to produce enough melatonin at the correct time. When I was younger, I was diagnosed with a severe Vitamin D deficiency, and was prescribed supplements. Vitamin supplements are easily available over the counter now, so if you do find it hard to sleep because of your lack of melatonin, then I recommend grabbing some next time you go past the chemist. (Just make sure to take them before midday, as you don't want to produce melatonin at the wrong time.)

A lot of us are guilty of using our phones and computers close to bedtime – me included – and although the blue light radiating from these devices doesn't contain Vitamin D, it can trick our brains into thinking that it does. So, if you have to use your phone late at night, then make sure to turn the brightness down – or even better, use night mode. Night mode is designed specifically so that the light emitting from your device will be warmer in colour. Warm, orange light is a lot more soothing for your eyes before bed than harsh yellow, blue, or white light.

Hopefully, after doing all that prep work, our minds will be ready to initiate sleep. But if we find ourselves lying in bed unable to switch off the brain just yet, then there are still some things we can do to help send it on its way.

For those who struggle with anxiety or depression, the night can be the worst time of day. It's that time when the world falls away and all that's left is *you*, and you alone. All of the distractions disappear, and those worries that we've been supressing all day start to bubble to the surface of our minds, just waiting to pop the cork on that bottle of bedlam. We've worked hard to create the best possible environment for sleep, void of stimulus, and then our brains are reignited with the fire of fear. When we're already anxious, beginning to feel stressed about not being able to get to sleep turns into a negative cycle which is really hard to break, and calm down the mind. I know from experience that the harder we try and force ourselves to nod off, the harder it becomes to achieve.

When I'm stuck in one of these stress loops, I like to deploy a good old, tried-and-tested distraction technique. I don't advocate supressing negative thoughts and emotions in any way shape or form – but the night really isn't the best time to deal with them, simply because we're tired, and we don't have the mental energy to think as rationally as necessary. Instead, we can make a quick note of our worries, and in the morning, tackle them with all the energy and brain power we've got.

Some people find that reading is beneficial in bed; I used to recite the Fibonacci sequence in my head. Reading and counting have a particular rhythm to them, proven to help send us to sleep. For a while, the counting worked for me, but it got to a point that when I reached larger and larger numbers – I'd start to feel stressed again, as it would represent how long I'd been awake...

Now, instead, I recite song lyrics. It's been recommended that I should try listening to music to help me drift off, but I find that too stimulating, as my brain is constantly trying to figure out rhythms and chord progressions. Unlike counting numbers, lyrics aren't quantifiable in the same way, and for me this is the perfect level of activity that my brain needs to be distracted from my troubles, but not so engaged that I'm no longer restful. My all-time favourite song for this exercise is Billy Joel's *We Didn't Start the Fire*. Go on, give it a try. I dare you.

I have better quality sleep when I spend a little bit longer lying awake in bed with my eyes closed, rather than trying to force it upon myself when my body isn't ready. Let sleep come to you naturally. It can take months to train our brains to establish a new sleep routine, so don't give up if all your efforts haven't worked on Night One. Even if none of these things have helped you, that's okay. We're all different, and you just need to find a routine that works for you – one that gets you the opposite of going.

The link between Vitamin D and the autistic brain is one of the great tangible strategies regarding sleep. But there is still so much that needs to be done concerning other aspects of mental and physical health. Disrupted sleep is usually the first tell-tale sign of disturbance within our minds and bodies.

We tend to judge how healthy we are by our exteriors. As long as we're not in any physical pain, we don't think there is a problem. But mental health problems don't just spring out of nowhere. You don't wake up one day and find that you suddenly have depression. It takes months, even years to develop, which is why it is so important that we start practising prevention, instead of trying to find a cure when it's already established. Many people – like me – aren't even aware of what is happening until we reach crisis point. And if these conditions take months and years to develop, just think about how long they can take to treat.

I had absolutely no idea that anxiety was such an ongoing condition. Humans tend to have a baseline level of tolerance to stress. I'm not a complainer, but I am a creature of solitude, therefore the old 'talk it out' strategy has never been one that I've warmed to. I like to think that it's because I'm the reincarnation of a character from a 1930's silver screen Clark Gable movie. Instead of letting my stress escape safely through an hour-long rant to a friend, I quietly sit and simmer, until I completely bubble over. I never look anxious when I'm having a panic attack, as my autistic trait to mask is so deeply imbedded within me that it has become automatic to hide my feelings. As my emotions weren't visible, this allowed my angst to grow exponentially.

The first time I ever properly got anxious about something was when I was seven. I was worried that Father Christmas wouldn't be able to visit because of the recession. A year later, I was worried that the world was going to end because they were switching on the Large Hadron Collider for the very first time, which could have triggered the most powerful particle accelerator in the world to create tiny black holes and rip apart time and space as we know it. That same summer, I worried about whether or not there was going to be a nuclear war. I didn't even know whether or not I'd want to survive it. I wouldn't want to come out of a shelter and have to try and rebuild society. (I definitely don't have the skills for that. I've only recently built my first piece of flat-pack furniture.)

Three years later, my dad was diagnosed with cancer. 'If only we *had* all plunged into a black hole' I thought, 'he wouldn't have had to be ill in the first place'. Being autistic made me much more aware of what was happening in the world than my peers. I couldn't understand why the other children in the playground weren't bothered by the financial crash, or the war in Iraq. I thought that everyone was this anxious all the time too. Why *wouldn't* you be? There is so much to worry about.

I have spent my whole life teetering on the edge of sanity, always living in a state of fight or flight. This is partly due to me being autistic, but mostly due to bureaucrats wielding excessively large amounts of red tape. Some children are shy, nervous and apprehensive, and some are simply reckless. In order to save the lives of the reckless ones, warnings are plastered just about everywhere imaginable to try and protect them. The result of this is that the apprehensive group live in a state of perpetual terror.

On top of my autism and my already heightened senses, growing up in a world decorated with 'warning!' and 'danger!' signs put me in an everlasting state of red alertness. I was living in survival mode all the time. You have to admit that it is pretty intimidating to be greeted with 'Stop!' signs every time you want to go somewhere.

I was *never* going to tear across a road full of speeding traffic, or climb up onto some rickety scaffolding. What *I* needed when I was younger was for someone to tell me 'Don't worry Charlotte, most days, you probably *won't* die'.

Being brought up in a world that is always pointing out the danger that could be waiting for me around the next corner meant I was constantly waiting for the next bad thing to happen – because the world had already predicted it. Otherwise, it wouldn't be warning me with a great big sign. Will there be a loud bang? Will my dad die? Because I know at some point, those things will happen.

Putting my body under this kind of pressure, remaining on constant high alert, was obviously going to have an effect. An effect that reached much further than I could have possibly imagined.

From the age of seven to fourteen, my anxiety had just been invisible thoughts circulating round in my head. We tend to only fight what we can see, and I thought that if I couldn't see it, then it might just go away by itself. I had no idea that those thoughts could manifest themselves physically. It was called *mental* health for a reason, right? Because it was just in your head? I soon came to the painful realisation that anxiety and mental health was anything but invisible. For years, my head was so packed full of the pressures of having to mask and to be hypervigilant, that my physical health started to suffer.

As a 14-year-old, my resting heart rate was averaging 125 bpm. I couldn't sleep. I was always recovering from some kind of illness or infection. I stopped eating, because the slightest anxious thought would make me physically sick. I was constantly changing my shirt, as by the middle of the day it would be drenched in sweat. I was exhausted all the time, but even when I could sleep, I never felt rested. It was as if I was running a marathon every minute of the day. My anxiety was flying off the charts, and I was flying away with it. I was *too high to function.*

Like one great big Jenga tower, one little piece could knock the whole thing down. I wasn't expecting my unhealed traumas and anxiety to suddenly jump out of the woodwork and strike. And then, that bang – the one I'd been dreading / trying to ignore / waiting for – finally went off.

Right Said Freud

Unexpressed emotions never die. They are buried alive and will come forth in later years in uglier ways.

Sigmund Freud

Playlist for Chapter 9

Wheels of the Machine, The Darkness

Broken Stones, Paul Weller

Those Simple Things, Right Said Fred

The Whole of the Moon, The Waterboys

River, Joni Mitchell

Vienna, Billy Joel

Metamorphosis, Philip Glass

Even the Darkness Has Arms, The Barr Brothers

Hmm. Tricky.

Very tricky.

Do I prioritise wheel diameter over the traction of the tyres? Or top speed over the addition of turbocharge? These are just some of the many things you have to consider when purchasing your first wheelchair... Okay, maybe not – but a car fanatic can dream, right?

Most teenagers long for the day when they finally get to learn to drive. That feeling of complete and utter freedom, sitting at the wheel for the first time, is truly unbeatable. I guess you could call me lucky, because I got all the excitement of learning to drive slightly earlier than my friends. Honestly, it wasn't quite as glamorous as I had hoped. There was no freedom, or even a glimmer of adventure behind my wheel. Or I should say, wheels.

As I sat there in the shop, test-driving all the different models, I couldn't help but replay the last few months of my life over and over again, trying to figure out how I had got here. Me, a fourteen-year-old girl who was a competitive dancer and figure skater, was test-driving wheelchairs.

Little did I know that what had seemingly only just begun to take over my body had, in fact, been rampaging through it for years.

I barely even noticed what had started happening to me, because it was all so gradual. It began with muscle soreness after any form of exertion. Being a competitive figure skater at the time, this feeling was normal, and is something that all athletes put up with. I also felt drowsier around this time – but the competition season had just ended, so that was to be expected. I had fallen in one of my last practises and had started walking with a limp, causing me to turn out my leg at an almost 90-degree angle. I had to use a crutch for a while; but that single crutch turned into two. I hadn't broken anything, so I just thought I needed to let my body recover from the fall in whatever way it needed too. I was sleeping for around 15 hours per day, but when I woke, I felt as if I hadn't been to bed at all.

My muscles kept getting sorer, and my lie-ins kept getting longer, and soon I became completely numb to it all. I couldn't remember what painlessness felt like. The day I realised that this wasn't the fault of my fall was the day everything changed.

It hit me at six o'clock one Tuesday morning. I woke up, intending to get out of bed to get ready for school, but I couldn't move. It was like my body had been shackled to my bed. No matter how much I forced my limbs, the most movement I could muster was a twitch in my left arm. It felt like I had been poisoned.

At the time I weighed eight stone, but I felt like I weighed 18. I felt encased in cement. I tried to sit up, but I was in such immense pain that I could only prise myself up onto my elbows. Just doing that left me breathless. I was burning up one minute, feeling frozen the next. My head was dizzy, and I could barely see across my bedroom. I vividly remember the sunrise seeping through my window, like hot, molten lava slowly trickling down a volcano. 'There aren't any active volcanos in the Midlands', I thought, so it had to be a dream. But it wasn't a dream. I was definitely awake, and I was living a nightmare.

I rolled onto my side, which felt like I was crushing my lungs, and I struggled for breath. I dangled my legs over the bed, and forced myself to stand up. The window ledge broke my fall as I found that my feet could no longer support my own weight. I had no control over my legs as they began to jolt and spasm. Feeling helpless, lying there on the floor, I didn't even have the energy to cry or shout for help. Thankfully my mum heard me fall. She rushed into my room, but I could only whisper two slurred words to her. 'Everything. Hurts.'

I did the worst thing imaginable and consulted Dr Google. Naturally, he said that I'd be dead by next Sunday afternoon. My mum did the sensible thing however, and made an actual doctor's appointment, with someone whose name bore no resemblance to an internet search engine. He couldn't find anything wrong with me and suggested that I had a bad virus. My mum then took me to a chiropractor to try and help with my muscle aches, but he could barely lay a finger on me without causing me to cry out in pain.

We went back to my GP, and since he didn't know what to do with me, he referred me to a paediatrician. She suspected that I had pernicious anaemia, and proceeded to take pints of my blood to check. During my consultation, the paediatrician mentioned another illness that might be the culprit if my results came back clear for anaemia, but I thought I'd misheard. A 'completely undetectable illness' sounded like something that belonged in a science fiction film. It was Myalgic Encephalomyelitis. (The illness, not the film.)

This illness also goes by another name, Chronic Fatigue Syndrome. This title doesn't really do it justice. Calling M.E 'Chronic Fatigue Syndrome' is like calling Dementia 'Chronic Forgetfulness Syndrome'. The word Mylagic means muscle pain, and Encephalomyelitis means inflammation of the brain, nerves, and spinal cord.

RIGHT SAID FREUD   175

The cause of M.E. is unknown, but some theories include viral and bacterial infections, problems with the immune system, hormone imbalances, and post-traumatic stress. I hadn't had a recent infection, nor had I had problems with my immune system or hormones, and it couldn't be post-traumatic stress, because that sounded ridiculous.

The cause of such an illness couldn't be down to stress and trauma. How could it be? Surely it had to be something severely life threatening? Not that I wanted to have a life-threatening illness, but there had to be a bloody good explanation as to why I was all of a sudden in crippling amounts of pain.

In the few months whilst I waited for my results, my condition got drastically worse. It was far too late to halt my physical deterioration now, as my body had already hit crisis point. My world was getting smaller and smaller, whilst everyone else's around me continued to expand – at somewhat an alarming rate by comparison.

My tiredness turned into exhaustion; my pain turned into torture. No matter how much I slept, the fatigue never went away. Most people can push through the feeling of being tired, but *fatigue* is an entirely different experience – it is the epitome of weakness. I couldn't even cope with lying down and watching tv, as even that required too much cognition. I felt like I had been anaesthetised, and because of this, I struggle to recall even the most poignant of moments from this time. My sweet sixteenth, my prom, all of the things that matter as a teenager, were all lost in a void of suffering.

The pain radiated into every one of my muscles, and my joints became ever more inflamed. My legs felt like they were made of glass, ready to shatter at the slightest pressure. I couldn't even brush my own teeth anymore, let alone wash my hair, or get dressed by myself. There were some days when I couldn't lift my fork from my plate to my mouth. It felt like my body had started to shut down. By this time, I needed 24-hour round-the-clock care.

To my utter disbelief, my test results came back clear. Every single one of them. I wasn't dying. I was stressed.

To understand how stress can affect your body's chemistry, you need to understand something called the hypothalamic-pituitary-adrenal axis. (Let's call it the HPA axis for short; you're welcome.) The HPA axis is a complex network that controls our body's reaction to stress, and regulates a lot of body processes, such as the immune response, digestion, energy, and our mood. These processes are controlled through connections between two glands in our nervous system, the hypothalamus and pituitary, and our adrenal glands. These glands produce hormones, and when these hormones get unbalanced, many body systems and functions, like the immune response, can be negatively affected.

It seemed that all my emotional pain had turned physical overnight. I felt pathetic. (I reasoned: if only I had talked it out, and hadn't masked my trauma for so long, maybe I wouldn't be in this mess? There was no one to blame but myself.) I was told by my teachers that mental health was just in your head – and to some extent they were right. Only now it was also in my neck, my back, my arms, fingers, legs, and toes. M.E. brought a whole new meaning to the phrase crippling anxiety.

I was told that there wasn't a cure for M.E., and that I had to completely change my lifestyle to manage this new chapter of my life. I had to strip my activities back to the basics. I had to pace myself, and I could only focus on the essentials, like eating and getting washed and dressed. All my hobbies had to go – not that I was physically able to do them anyway – and I had to stop doing anything that exhausted me. So, pretty much everything. From that moment on, I felt like my life was stuck on pause. I was only able to see the crescent, never the whole of the moon. It was like I was living behind a glass screen. I could still see everything flashing before me, but I couldn't touch it, no matter how hard I tried to break through that glass, and trying only reminded me of just how incapacitated I had become. I remember one doctor asked me how old I was, and I couldn't tell him. I simply didn't know anymore. I had to work it out. That's how disconnected I felt from my peers, I no longer felt my age.

I was advised to take the pressure off attending school, but I was determined to get my qualifications like everybody else. Looking back at photographs from me at that time, I honestly don't know how I managed it; it very nearly killed me, physically and mentally. But somehow, I did it. I did it all.

The only way I could manage leaving the house was if I was in a wheelchair. My wheelchair gave me the mileage I didn't have in my legs, which allowed me to use the few scraps of energy that I had left for schoolwork.

With the help of my newly-appointed sensory occupational therapist, we put together a timetable which allowed me to attend school in person for four hours a week, whilst completing the rest online and by having tutors come to the house. This meant that I was still able to see my friends and to touch base with school, without it draining me for the rest of the week. This was when energy became my new currency.

The value of energy is extremely high, and the conversion rate is abysmal. When you have M.E., everything you do has a price tag. Some things, like going to the park, charge a smaller fee than going to go to a gig with friends. Going to school was a very expensive activity, hence only being able to attend for four hours a week. My whole life was spent working out if I could afford to do certain things, so that they didn't leave me in crippling amounts of debt.[1] At this point, my sensory occupational therapist was more like a financial advisor.

Think of your energy like your phone battery. Most people's bodies run on 90 to 100 per cent battery life most of the time. By the end of each day, they will probably have progressively dipped down to around a 20 or 10 per cent charge. They plug themselves in overnight, and wake up in the morning fully charged again. If you have M.E., your charger is broken, and you are only able to reach around 40 to 50 per cent worth of charge to begin with. You drop to around 10 per cent within a matter of hours. You then have to do *absolutely nothing* whilst you recuperate, so that you

---

1. Literally.

can make it to the end of the day, and you go to bed knowing that in the morning you will feel as if you haven't slept at all.

Even after being bullied, self-harming, and my parent's separation, the first time I ever want to school in my wheelchair was, without a doubt, the worst day of my life. I didn't tell any of my friends beforehand, simply because I didn't know how to. I soon went from being the unnoticeable girl who did everything to avoid attention to the girl everyone was talking about. I no longer had a personality, because all anyone ever saw was the chair. I was no longer known as the girl who was an amazing ice-skater, but the girl who was disabled. I just wanted to have normal teenage problems: does that boy like me? What's the dress code for the prom afterparty? Not: will my wheels fit through this doorway?

Before the chair, I could mask my differences – which, ironically, was one of the reasons why I ended up in it – but now my differences were exposed to everyone. I got bored of people asking me over and over again why I was even in a wheelchair, so I started getting creative with my answers. I told one Year Nine student that I was higher up the evolutionary chain than everyone else, and that I had evolved wheels. I told a couple of Year Sevens that I had fallen off a unicorn, and I told my fellow classmates that I was only in it for the benefits and the parking. After all, every cloud has a silver lining.

Surprisingly enough, my peers weren't my biggest issue. Apart from a handful of respectful teachers, the school staff had a very unhelpful perspective on my condition. They viewed my illness as a pure fabrication of my mind, despite all the recent research showing that scientists could clearly make a distinction between the way M.E. and healthy immune cells process stress (thanks to the HPA axis) and the devastating effects this has on the body. As we know, our emotions can be in control of how our hormones are produced, so when our body becomes used to a state of heightened anxiety, it starts to recognise that response as an immediate threat, causing cells to start attacking each other, like any other auto/neuro-immune disease.

These were the same teachers who told me that bullying was character building, and that mental health didn't exist. One told me that if I was too ill to come to school, then I simply shouldn't be there, and that because I was disabled, I shouldn't even try and bother getting myself a future. Fun attitude: perhaps they should directly hand me over the percentage of their tax bill that I would inevitably be receiving from the benefits office for the rest of my life? That same teacher also refused to move their lessons to a downstairs classroom, forcing me to crawl up three flights of stairs on my hands and knees to attend class. (Only on the days when I had the energy to do this, as on the days when I didn't, I was left awkwardly staring at the school receptionist for an hour, whilst everyone else had their lesson.)

Soon after senior management got hold of this information, they deemed that having a student who regularly crawled up the stairs on their hands and knees, who relied on someone else to push their wheelchair, *and* who had slower cognitive decision-making abilities made them an obstruction to other pupils. I was now deemed a fire hazard. So... *I* was the problem here?

Despite there being two other wheelchair users in the school at the time, it took over 12 months to have a ramp installed. (It was fitted four months before I left.) For years, we were only ever able to access a portion of the school site, as even the ground floor had steps in certain places.

When my mum enquired about me attending sixth form, the response from the Head was that, due to the location of the sixth form centre, combined with my slower cognitive processing, they wouldn't even entertain the idea. 'Over my dead body' is the phrase that stuck out in both my Mum's and occupational therapist's minds from that meeting.

All in all, I would describe this systematic collapse as a collective failure of imagination.

I traded in every scrap of dignity I had, just to be able to access the same education my friends were receiving. Thankfully this just spurred me on to show them all what I was always capable of achieving. But that right there is the dangerous attitude towards mental health that has been preached for decades.

'Mental health' is anything but a fabrication. Poor mental health leads people to self-harm, become physically disabled, and even end their own lives. When I first heard the term 'toxic positivity', I was confused. Positivity is a good thing, right?

Phrases such as 'just stop worrying!' or 'just be happy!' can silence negative emotions to the point where we begin to feel ashamed of them. We start to put unnecessary pressure on ourselves to be happy all the time, when in reality, that's an unrealistic goal. Toxic positivity demands we only think of positive outcomes, regardless of tragedy, which can bury our negative emotions – ultimately making them a lot louder and scarier to confront.[2]

Telling someone to 'stop worrying' or to 'just think happy thoughts' is like watching somebody drowning and telling them to just keep swimming. When somebody is *drowning*, you leap into the water to try and save them. You act on the spur of the moment

---

2. A bit like running into Brian Blessed in a library.

and throw them a lifejacket, because *they need help*. The important thing to remember is that people who can swim still drown. All the time. It's not because they don't know how to swim, but simply that right now, they can't stay above the water.

The link between mental and physical health was first identified by the founder of psychoanalysis, Sigmund Freud. In the 19th century, Freud and his protégé Josef Breuer worked together on one of the very first cases of psychoanalysis, featuring the patient Bertha Pappenheim. Around the age of 20, her father began to fall seriously ill, and in turn, she started displaying physical symptoms alongside her anxiety and depression that could not be linked to a single cause. A few years later, her father died, and her condition drastically deteriorated. She suffered from anxiety, memory loss, occasional blindness, deafness, and seizures. This led to her being diagnosed with 'hysteria'. Little did Freud and Breuer know that their treatment of Bertha Pappenheim was to change the course of therapy forever.

They used an adaptation of the now commonly known therapy practice of hypnosis. Before Bertha, hypnosis was used to try and correct a person's behaviours, but Breuer and Freud used it in an entirely different way. They thought that by helping her to unfold her supressed memories and thoughts, her unconscious trauma would become conscious, and by confronting the mental stress that was causing her physical pain, her symptoms would start to cease. As soon as she managed to make her ongoing unconscious pain heard, she began to make a recovery.

Josef managed to treat a lot of Bertha's severe symptoms, but some remained unhealed. There is a much controversy about why some of her symptoms didn't dissipate, but I believe that because mental and physical health are intertwined, you cannot treat one set of symptoms without respecting the other. Perhaps his approach solely relied on focusing on her mental state, and not relieving any of the physical symptoms that ran in tandem with her mental condition?

After much conflict, Freud and Breuer eventually published her case under the alias 'Anna O', and Bertha was able to start living her life again. After her treatment ended, she experienced more episodes – but therapy is something that needs to be ongoing, and is never just a quick fix. However, her re-emerging symptoms later subsided, and she went on to become one of the most influential feminist leaders of her time.

Sigmund Freud concluded that physical symptoms are often the manifestation of deeply repressed negative emotions. I did some more digging into this potential origin of my illness and the connection between the brain and the body, and it finally became clear to me. My M.E. was caused by post-traumatic stress – which meant that I could attempt to do something about it. Yes, I could see a chiropractor weekly to address my joint and muscle pain, but without addressing the root cause of the problem as well as the symptoms, I never had a hope of recovering.

I desperately wanted to get back to living the life I'd had. I was stuck, grieving for the loss of a girl I didn't know I'd ever see again. I missed the sound of my skates carving and crunching up the ice, and seeing the sketches they would leave behind on its surface. These sketches were always delicately rough and undefined, without rules and limitations – they were free.

My wheels squeaked. Their sketches were always inexpressive: the same distance apart, and they usually just meant I had inadvertently rolled through a puddle.

I started by finding a way to acknowledge my pain, and no longer be frightened of it. I had spent years masking my feelings, because I didn't think that they were things I was allowed to feel. That stiff-upper-lip mentality that runs through a Brit's veins is actually a very damaging one.

By dissecting the thoughts behind the feelings, we can really start to see the evidence[3] for why we feel the things we feel. This requires us to *give ourselves the right to notice negative thoughts.* If you journal or keep a diary, you probably make a note of these emotions already. This is a great technique, as it can help us to start normalising those thoughts, so they're less shocking when we begin to actually feel them. But the thing that I do most to train my brain into acknowledgment is to get creative. Most of the poetry and music that I write is a manifestation of some kind of tantrum or trauma. I love taking the sirens of my pain and give them a new voice: one that's softer, more forgiving; one that has the same quality of being able to silence me, but in a beautiful, rather than an ugly way.

Talking of ugliness, that is exactly how being in a wheelchair made me feel. Mainly because, whenever I caught someone glancing over at me, my pain was reflected back in their face in the form of fear. I underestimated the effect that my sudden transformation would have on my classmates. People started avoiding me, distancing themselves, and pretending that I didn't exist; and at first, I had no idea why. I was confused, upset, and I felt more isolated than I

---

3. Or in some cases, the lack of evidence.

had ever been before. But then I came across a term that explained their fear.

Stigmas surface when people are ignorant. That misunderstanding then turns into fear. Too many people are scared of seeing someone in a wheelchair because they don't know how to approach them. Think of how scary it is for the person who is actually disabled! I didn't want to make people feel like they had to hide or cower away from me in the corridors. I also didn't want everyone to throw their arms round me and become my new best friend. I wanted to do something that meant I was approachable enough to spark a conversation about disability, without having to become the PM in the process. Really, all I wanted was not to be an object of fear.

I was just a few weeks away from spending my first ever Christmas without skating on an outdoor rink, one of my favourite activities to do at this time of year. Another one of my favourite things about Christmas is the lights. My mum and I set off on our annual Christmas tradition of driving round all the hideous, garish and tackily decorated houses in our neighbourhood. They did not disappoint.

There were elves, happily being electrocuted on people's front lawns. There were Christmas trees, drenched branch-to-branch in fake snow and polystyrene. There was even a display of carol-singing snowmen, conducted by a storm trooper. What that has to do with Christmas I will never know, but it gave us some light relief after the previous house, and its harrowing scene of an inflatable Father Christmas having it off with a reindeer.

All bestiality aside, this gave me an idea. I thought that if people were going to make themselves miserable just by looking at me, I could at the very least try and make them smile, so they would be less afraid of my disability in particular, and all disability in general. I got my mum to thread fairy lights in and out of the spokes of the wheels on my chair, and she cable tied a couple of battery packs under the wheel arches. This was around the time the National Oceanography Centre was trying to rename the UK's new exploration ship through a public vote, and the name 'Boaty McBoat Face' was a popular contender.[4] So we bought some glittery letters and stuck them on the back of my chair, to spell out 'Wheely McWheel Face'. We managed to make something pretty out of something shitty, and it certainly did the job.

For the first time in months, people actually smiled at me when I rolled down the hallways. Some even laughed – but they laughed with me this time.

---

4. Disappointingly, they went for the sensible option, and named the ship after Sir David Attenborough.

Shortly after that same Christmas, a friend of mine sadly passed away. It was a very strange time, and no one really knew how to react or behave. She was the first person I met who truly understood what it was like to be so different from everyone else. Like me, she was also a new wheelchair user, and we used to have races across the playground. We even invented a brand-new sport, wheelchair jousting.[5] We hardly ever spoke about our illnesses, as there was always a mutual understanding which meant we never had to explain a thing. We could just be ourselves, without having to justify our existences. Although I only knew her for a short time, our circumstances bonded us.

I had extinguished my Christmas fairy lights just weeks before she died, but people needed to be smiling again. Not out of a disregard for the tragedy, but out of celebration for her life. Besides, I knew she would approve. She used to say that I brought the much-needed sparkle to the sanitorium. Not only was it what I needed, but it was what everyone else needed too. Reinstating those lights helped spark a much-needed conversation about

---

5. Yet to be recognised by the Paralympics.

disability and mental health between my peers and teachers, and I can only hope that I shone a light into the darkness at that incredibly difficult time.

I think we can all agree, having gone through a pandemic together, that disarray can bring out the worst in people. But it also brings out the best. It's easy for me to get lost in all the negativity I experienced at school, but there were also people who fought for me when I wasn't strong enough to keep doing so. There were people who made it possible for me to achieve my goals; people who knew how wrongly I was being treated, who weren't afraid to do the right thing. After I left school, my mental and physical health deteriorated further due to the fallout, so I was unable to complete my higher education at the time. But in retrospect, I am delighted to say that I have now started my A-Levels, having passed my first one last year in 2022. I didn't have to go back to education, no one forced me. It was my choice. No matter how embarrassed or stupid doing my A-Levels makes me feel (when according to my age I should be graduating from university by now) I'm never going to give up on myself, no matter how long it takes – and that's partly because a few select teachers didn't give up either. Yes,

I'm doing it for myself, but I am also doing it for them. Thank you to my Head of Year, Design & Technology teacher, Art & Photography teacher, Biology teacher, and all my home tutors, for believing that I could make it. Look!

We feel as though we are being judged if we discuss our vulnerabilities, like they somehow make us weak. We grow to become ashamed of them, and we start ignoring them. We're disgraced by their virtues. But we need to be kind to our emotions because they can be just as damaged as we are. Love is blind. Fear suffers from paralysis. Depression is mute. Pride is tasteless. Lust has Alzheimer's, and arousal has incredibly poor impulse control.

I know how easy it is to become engulfed by the prison of our own minds... but being able to accept all those dark thoughts that we wish we didn't have is the most important step in overcoming them. As I mentioned earlier, in the same way that it's unrealistic to expect every day to be a good one, it is also unrealistic to expect every day to be bad – because there is no such thing as a 'bad' day. There are days when you have to try harder to be stronger, but I would in no way describe that courageous act as bad.

The more we ignore and become scared of our negative thoughts, the more they demand our attention. Our bodies will always find a new way to get us to listen, so we mustn't neglect them. After years of people telling me to stop being anxious and sad – but not actually telling me *how* – I started shutting out the signs of poor mental health. Despite my turmoil, I had been so incredibly lucky with who raised me, where I was educated, and everyone else that I had met along the way that I felt too privileged to admit to having a dark side. I felt ashamed, guilty, and unworthy of help. I didn't think I deserved it. But the truth is, asking for help isn't giving up. It is *refusing* to give up. It doesn't matter who or where you are; just like physical health, mental health doesn't discriminate.

I used to be able to regularly get hold of the glue that I would use to stick myself back together. I would throw myself into a new obsession, or murderous docudrama, in the hope of avoiding the real-life drama taking place inside. If a couple of pieces of me dropped off during the year, I'd make a temporary fix. A string of distractions. But one day, the glue just didn't arrive.

I woke up in a bed surrounded by all my broken pieces, bewildered as to why there were more shattered shards of me than expected.

I ended up in a wheelchair because I didn't listen to my body. Every headache, every absence from school was just my body's way of trying to tell me to get help. Looking back, I can see that my poor neglected physical self had been trying to get me to listen for years – and in the end, the only way it could bring me to a standstill was by taking away the things I loved. I once felt incredibly resentful towards my body, as I hated how it appeared to fail on me. But now, I feel compassion for it. I realised that it never wanted to ruin my life, it only wanted to help me. I will never underestimate it again.

I managed to turn my breakdown into a breakthrough. I took those same broken pieces lying all around me, and I rebuilt myself, creating a being that was even stronger than the first. By strengthening my mind, I have strengthened my body.

The metamorphosis I have undergone in the last few years has not been about growing up and getting older, but about getting better. If I look back at what has really changed physically in the last eight years since falling ill, other than the fact I now have a smile, not much seems to have changed at all. I still use my wheelchair. I still use my crutches. 'Simple' tasks, such as breathing and walking, that are usually automatic and taken for granted, are still entirely conscious processes for me that I am always aware of. The way my feet fall on the ground, the slight twist of my knee, the depth of my breath when I'm struggling for air. I still have to fight to exist every single day. But on the inside, I have regenerated into an entirely different entity.

What has changed? The way I perceive the world around me, my understanding for others' circumstances, my acceptance of the insecurities in the ones I love, and the ones I hate. The way I talk, hurt, the way I love. I could never have imagined how grateful I would come to feel after losing everything, or that I'd even feel grateful at all. In a strange turn of events, it could possibly be one of the best things that ever happened to me.

There is a painless solution to my life. There's a painless solution to everyone's life. I could just do nothing. If I did nothing, then sure, I'd be in less physical pain, and I would probably have some more energy; but I wouldn't have anything to spend that energy on. Instead of fearing my pain, I use it as my reminder that I am alive – which is an incredible gift that I once took for granted.

One of the hardest things to do is to love a body that doesn't work. Except I've learnt that mine *does* work, just for a different purpose: to give me the strength I didn't have to be able to live.

Me and my body have made amends, and our deal is a pretty sweet one. My pain isn't going to stop me from doing the things that I love, but it will make me stop and think about what is causing it, and we have a mutual understanding that I need to take that pain as a sign to slow things down. I don't see my M.E. as an illness anymore, but as a best friend who is always looking out for me.

At the start of this book, we talked about what success really means. It will mean something different to everyone. During the time I have spent writing this book, I have found my definition. I'm ashamed to say that it was quite obvious, yet somehow, I missed it.

For me, giving my pain a purpose will be my success story. Even if only one person finds what I have written helpful, *all* my misfortune would have been worth it.

Because in the end, pain is the only thing that can save you.

Meldrew

To every man is given the key to the gates of heaven; the
same key opens the gates of hell.
Buddhist proverb, favoured by Richard Feynman

Playlist for Chapter 10

Dandy In The Underworld, T. Rex

Monkey Man, The Rolling Stones

Two Tribes, Frankie Goes To Hollywood

Monkey In Your Soul, Steely Dan

The Lovecats, The Cure

The Spirit Of Radio, Rush

Piano Man, Billy Joel

When the Going Gets Tough, the Tough Get Going, Billy Ocean

There's this old man. I've known him most my life. I know you're supposed to treat your elders with grace and respect, but this one's a prick. His name is Meldrew. I don't really know how old he is; I've never asked him because I don't really care. He is all alone. He doesn't have any family. He doesn't even have any friends. Because he's a prick. It's obvious why he's alone.

I used to think that if I was nice to him, then he'd be nice to me. (Like that old saying from the Bible about an eye for a pie and a tooth for a sleuth?) I did try being nice to him once, I really did. But in the end, we got on together about as well as Jesus and Judas Iscariot at the disciples' reunion bash.

Normally, when I meet someone that mawks[1] me off, I simply remind myself that one day, eventually, they will be dead. There is one slight complication with that thought process when it comes to Meldrew. Quite a big complication actually; he lives inside my brain.

---

1. Mawk – someone who acts like a prat.

'Life is like a box of chocolates. You never know what you're going to get'... and it can leave you feeling sick.

Anxiety is a beast of a complex nature. It can impact your mental and physical health in ways you didn't deem possible. It comes in a plethora of different forms, say, generalised day-to-day anxiety, social phobia, or OCD. I'm lucky enough to have all three of those – not to brag, but I'm what doctors refer to as a triple threat.

Meldrew is my inner chimp. My internal monologue. My doubts, pessimism, and anxiety personified. He is my alter ego.

I say *alter* ego, but really, he's just my actual ego. I essentially live with the brain of an 84-year-old man in the body of a 23-year-old woman. Needless to say, it's very confusing. I think that's why I despise him so much, because we are frightfully similar. When I say that I'm frightfully similar to a cranky old geezer, I don't mean that I hate gay marriage, foreigners, and McDonalds. I love all of those things. I mean more along the lines that I hate predictive text and gangster rap.[2]

---

2. If you hadn't already thought that I'd lost the plot entirely, you probably have now. I promise I don't dabble in crack. I just have one bastard of a monkey in my head.

You may be reading this and thinking that none of this will apply to you, because you're not autistic. You probably think that you are in control of your mind all the time. If that's the case, then why did you drink that extra glass of wine last night? Why did you eat those biscuits, even though you're on a diet? There's a reason they put the chocolate right next to the checkouts, and it has nothing to do with autism.

In which case, why am I talking about it?

Like it or not, everyone has a Meldrew. *Everyone* has an inner monologue. Sure, your internal voice may not be represented by a hateful octogenarian, but the principles are the same. It is responsible for all those thoughts that you wish your subconscious didn't have. Your chimp acts impulsively, without consideration for any consequences. It's greedy, self-obsessed, and a total pain in the arse.

A lot of people think that 'mental health' doesn't apply to them, because it's just for people with raging anxiety and depression. But the fact is, every single person with a brain has mental health, in the exact same way that everyone who has a body has physical health. We are all told that a good diet of whole foods and exercise is great for our physique, but our brain is arguably the most important organ in our body, and few of us are taught how to look after it.

People miss the warning signs of mental health problems because they seem so insignificant. We should be teaching people how to recognise those early signs, so we can prevent poor mental health from getting out of control – instead of acting when it is too late. Believe it or not, there is an incredibly fine line between feeling slightly anxious and having a diagnosable condition. As we discussed in the previous chapter, I didn't listen to those warning signs, and I'm still paying the price for my ignorance and denial.

Professor Steve Peters was the first to introduce 'The Chimp Paradox',[3] the idea that there are two distinct parts of our 'thinking' brains; they both lie on the brain's outer edge, known as the cortex. Peters defines our chimp as one part, and our human function as the other. The *prefrontal cortex* is where we find our human function. This part of the brain is where we think rationally and make decisions based on evidence. Our chimp lives in the *limbic system* and acts purely on emotion. This means that our chimp won't look at the context of a situation before making up its mind, and will often jump to drastic conclusions.

These two parts of our brain lurk side by side and work independently. They would get along fine if they worked in the

---

3. https://chimpmanagement.com/books-by-professor-steve-p eters/the-chimp-paradox/

same way – but they don't. So, we have the potential for a battle commencing in our minds at any time. Think of it as if the brain is a jungle. We have our chimp living happily in its natural habitat, and then there's our human function, which is trying to survive in, well... a jungle.

I'm painting the chimp in a bad light here, but it's actually an integral part of how we as a species have survived this long. Our chimp acts on our emotions, so more often than not, it will receive information before any other part of your brain. This is great when we're being chased by a lion, as our chimp will instantly fling us into a state of fight or flight, so we can run away. But sometimes our chimp perceives an attack even when there isn't one – which is why we say and do things in arguments that we later regret, and why we can start to develop anxiety.

So why don't we just ignore our chimp's urges? Well: in a fight between a chimp and a human, who wins? I think we can all agree that it's the chimp.

A chimp is much more powerful than a human, so there is no point in trying to wrestle it. Instead, we must learn to *parent* it. You are responsible for when your chimp decides to kick off, and it's your job to train it. Training it requires a lot of strength, but it is possible. When done effectively, our chimp will have the capacity to be our best friend, instead of our worst enemy. We've already established its power, so think about what we would be able to achieve if we used that power to its full advantage!

Parenting the chimp requires taking the time to let it speak its mind. Don't just ignore it, as it will only start rattling the bars of its monkey cage more angrily, till we give it the attention it desires. You'll find that your chimp gets exhausted quickly, so let it out, to run its course. (Just be careful who's around when you let your chimp out. My mum often says that when she's trying to reason with my anxiety, she finds herself talking directly to Meldrew. She knows that I'm not the one who needs opposing, so there's no point in trying to reason with me: she needs to speak directly to Meldrew.) Getting your chimp to listen to you can be a long process, but the more you teach it, the more you can start re-routing its thought patterns. Your chimp just needs guidance.

Before we start training our chimp, it's important that we learn how it reacts, so we know what will set it off and what will help calm it down. Cats, playing the piano, and watching snooker are the things that help calm my chimp down – an eclectic mix, I know. But as well as these things, my chimp also likes it when I'm upset, anxious, and doubtful. Our chimps are lazy, so feeding off negative emotions is the easiest way to manipulate us to get what they want.

Our minds contain all sorts of dark corners and winding alleyways, out of which the chimp is just waiting to pounce. It waits until we feel safe, and therefore at our most vulnerable. Being anxious about material things is one thing – but experiencing anxiety over things that have no real shape or form is arguably much more terrifying. Through all of the social challenges that I've faced, including relentless bullying and abuse, I can say with the utmost confidence that there is nothing more frightening than having to fight your own mind.

Back when I was at school, I was completely unaware that anxiety had begun to take control of my life. I put myself under immense pressure because I was a music scholar. Being expected to be one of the best meant that settling for anything less than perfection didn't feel like an option. I didn't want to let down the people who supposedly thought I was good enough. I became terrified of making a mistake, for fear that I was not. I started punishing myself, in all sorts of creative ways, every time I played a wrong note.

I have always doubted my abilities in anything that I was supposedly good at, because being naturally good at something was such an *unnatural* feeling to me. Compared to my friends and my brother, I had always been bad at everything everyone else was able to do – like having a simple conversation. So, when something came along that I was good at, it was very hard to accept.

I thought that the only reason they made me a music scholar was to be nice to me (like how I only got my Grade Eight on drums was because I was twelve and had sparkly drumsticks). Yet, despite not believing in my ability, music was the one thing that made me feel good about myself. It was how I communicated and expressed my emotions, and if I didn't have that, then I wouldn't have anything.

I loved music, I really did, but I *didn't* love performing in front of people. I get the worst cases of stage fright in existence. Before every school concert, I would starve myself, for up to a week, so that it was physically impossible for me to be sick on stage. My anxiety was quite literally gut-wrenching. I spent many a concert interval on the cusp of chunder, begging not to have to go through the same painful process again in the second half.

I didn't know that by becoming a music scholar, I had inadvertently signed myself up to be one of the school's performing monkeys. I have never wanted to take centre stage and be in the spotlight. I am quite happy as a small cog in a bigger machine; I get just as much satisfaction and sense of accomplishment out of that feeling.

I was told that I would never be a musician if I couldn't perform in front of people.

I now know this isn't the case – but at the time, Meldrew chose to believe it. If I couldn't do something I loved, then I'd have no hope in succeeding at anything else. Music was then added to the list of dreams-I-once-had, that would now be locked away. It made me never want to touch an instrument ever again. There was obviously no point. By now, I, myself, had become my own worst enemy. Every ounce of confidence and self-belief that I'd ever had was utterly demolished, and I had no idea how to begin to start the rebuilding process.

I left school with absolutely no aspiration or direction to do anything with my life. My cats were the only living things in front of whom I had ever played my music without feeling the urge to vomit. Not even my mum had heard me play, as I was too scared to ever turn up the volume on my keyboard. Sometimes I would play with my keyboard switched off completely. I think that the reason why I find it easier to connect with cats over humans is probably due to the fact that cats don't talk. (Or that they choose not to talk, I haven't quite decided yet, as we are all well aware that one day, inevitably, they will take over the world.) Despite their world domination plans, I feel less socially threatened by cats because they don't judge me. They will never care whether I mess up that bar of tricky triplets in the middle of a Chopin nocturne, or whether I play it perfectly. There is no level of expectation or pressure.

Meanwhile, whilst I was becoming the pied piper to super furry animals, my mum had heard through the grapevine about a local recording studio that might be able to give me the level of support I needed to play again. I was sceptical – and why wouldn't I be? No one had *ever* been willing to give me the support I needed. Not even places that promised me they could. To be honest, I thought she was joking. A recording studio? Seriously? It was bad enough having to compete with the sound of Meldrew mocking me every time I played the piano in my own living room, so why on earth would I want to immortalise that sound onto a CD? This was a terrible idea. The next thing I knew, she had gone to look round and take pictures for me, so I'd know what I might be walking into. She really wasn't joking at all.

The first photo showed a room with a large desk, and two men sitting around it. The desk was heavily clad with an array of switches and knobs; the sort of set up that any trigger-happy dictator would salivate over. The room was painted – well, to be frank – shoddily. None of the window ledges or skirting boards matched, and whoever had decorated around the light switches must have decided to use an electric toothbrush on full spin. But

– the door did have the carcass of a once functional cat flap, tentatively peeping through the many layers of congealed paint, and by now you should know that anything cat-related is enough to spark an interest for me.

The second picture was of a keyboard and a mini fridge.[4] The third photo was blurry, and seemed as though my mother had lost all ability to work a camera phone.[5] The final picture showed a drum kit that appeared to have been vajazzled with fairy lights. Anyone who knows me knows that the type of men who vajazzle drum kits with fairy lights are the very type of men I want to get to know.

The following week, I put on my gothy glad rags and prepared to leave the house. (Yes, I was indeed a goth, because, before I had the confidence to start socialising, I usefully discovered that being a goth was a natural form of human repellent.) I was really scared, and I had every right to be. I didn't know what to expect, or how they could help me and my anxiety. At best I thought that I'd turn up, see the piano, have instant flashbacks about school, break

---

4. Mum, this was a great shot, as I was able to scope out what sort of snacks I could store for my impending social bribes. Good work.

5. Sadly, all kudos gained for the fridge shot was instantly lost.

down, and never go back. It wouldn't have been my worst day out, and all in all there would be little to lose.

But I *didn't* break down at the sight of their piano. (Mainly because I couldn't see it; it was covered in books and knotted cables.) They seemed to understand everything I told them about the way I was.[6] There were no questions asked or any unjust justifications required. For the first time in my life, I was being *listened* to, not just heard.[7]

When I left, I felt slightly confused. Being understood was a brand-new experience for me. (Which was odd, as I had spoken to countless professionals and therapists beforehand, but none were like this pair.) I remember asking my mum what sort of specialist training and qualifications they had that meant they were so good at what they did. The answer stunned me. To my disbelief, they had had no training in autism or mental health whatsoever. Neither had studied psychology at university, and they were definitely not qualified therapists. They had learnt purely through experience, not at the back of some lecture hall

---

6. Despite one of them being from Somerset.

7. Remember the wise man I quoted back in Chapter 3? You're about to meet him!

with a textbook. They were just a couple of blokes who wanted to help me and many others.

They gave me so much hope in humanity, and made me realise that there were actually people out there who wanted to understand. It almost made me feel bad for having such a cynical view of the world. Had these men finally started to prove me wrong? I think they had.

Situated across the street sat a tiny, quaint café, used as the bait to lure me out of the house in the first place. My mum had heard that it was home to a couple of canoodling kittens, so she knew it would be the perfect bribe. I was born pre-programmed with cat-nav, so on entry, my eyes were instantly drawn to their location. To be fair, my cat-nav didn't have to work very hard to stake out the whereabouts of the first one, as he was sprawled over the doormat. To my surprise, the second was perched on the lid of an upright piano. A cat. On a piano. All I needed now was a snooker table, and I would be in paradise.

I got home that evening and started to process how surprisingly hopeful the day had been. It was the first time since leaving school that I felt any kind of faith in my future. As I serenaded my cats that night, it hit me. The piano in the café. I had always wondered why people bothered putting pianos in public places where you'd barely be able to hear them, but that's when the realisation came to me. Soundtracks are an essential part of films, TV shows, and our day-to-day lives. Whether sound comes from the radio station you're listening to, or the drum of rain hitting the windowpanes – our world is never truly silent. There is always some kind of background noise happening around you, even if you aren't consciously aware of it.

I had only ever played in front of expectant audiences before, never just as part of the background. Always, I was under pressure from being in the spotlight. This could all change now. I realised that if I played in front of people when I didn't think they were listening, or paying me any attention, maybe I *could just about do it?* Cafés are never silent, so people would hardly notice me playing at all. Pubs would be ideal too. Drunks aren't going to care about what sort of music they vomit to. Even if they started heckling me, my self-esteem would be fine with it, because they would be intoxicated, and all judgement would be skewed. (Also, if anyone did heckle me, I'm disabled, so it would technically be a hate crime.)

That was the dream right there. I had the motive, the means, and now the opportunity. As I sat playing to my cats, I became increasingly excited. But I had a long way to go. I hadn't even played in front of my family before, so the idea of playing in front of a room full of complete strangers was still terrifying. I knew that I had to start somewhere, and I decided that it should be with one of the two men whom I knew would understand. Specifically, the Somersetonian, as being born and bred in the land of cheddar and cider meant that he'd be an easy target for my social bribes.

The idea was odd – that someone would be getting paid to ignore me – but that's the only way that I could start building my confidence in a controlled way. Plus, it would be good training for what playing in a café would actually be like.[8] Unlike cat-nav, confidence was not something I was born with. Confidence is something we get only *after* we make that first initial jump. Think of it like a circle. The more we step out of that circle, the more our circle grows with us, and the more confident we become.

It took me many, many months, before I could even think about playing a single note in front of him, even whilst being ignored. As he was a total stranger, it took me a long time to build that trust that I've talked about previously in this book – to be able to consider him a 'safe' person. Due to my social anxiety, my mum had to attend every session with me, and for the first six months,

---

8. It takes a whole new level of concentration to be able to play well whilst somebody is loudly eating crisps and continuously quoting Alan Partridge at you.

all we did was chat. Well, my mum did most of the chatting. I sat and looked terrified.

Some days, depending on my energy levels, and whether or not I was sensory-overloaded that day, the goal would just be to get there, say hello, then come home again. You may think that just leaving the house to say hi to someone and then immediately return home seems like a waste of time. But those small steps are exactly what I needed to achieve, in order to begin to tackle my anxiety; in time, those small steps got bigger.

A considerable amount of time later, I finally felt comfortable enough when I was at the studio to send my mum into another room. I was now sufficiently confident to chat to the Somersetonian by myself, without her support. This was a huge step, as I knew that this meant I was closer to actually being able to play something in front of him. The thing about anxiety is: each step we take to tackle it will feel a lot bigger than the step before. So, the more steps we take, the tougher and harder it gets to face it.

The week that I sat behind the piano, he tried to hide his amazement. This was a big deal. The moment that I, he, and everyone had been waiting for had finally arrived. Little did he know, I wouldn't actually be switching the piano on that day. Or the day after that. But I still played the silent keys, and that's all that mattered.

I began to feel frustrated at my slow progress. I came home one evening, draped myself over the piano stool, and thought, 'I can't do this, I can't do this!' But that's when I noticed it.

'I can't do this'. Those very words *must* be false. I knew they were false, because I *could* play happily in front of my cats. I realised that what was stopping me playing in front of people has never been my ability, but *simply the narrative I told myself.* I told myself I couldn't play, so I couldn't play. I had had no idea that I'd been sabotaging myself the whole time. To my disbelief, the self-sabotage didn't stop there.

I realised that by not having any self-belief for all these years, I was defending myself from ever having to play in front of anyone. No one wants to listen to someone who can't play very well. So, by telling myself I was bad at music, I was protecting myself from doing the things that scared me the most. I had been surrendering myself to Meldrew this whole time. Self-sabotage had become my coping mechanism.

I didn't want to be scared – but I had to re-evaluate what scared me more. If self-sabotage meant that I would forever live an unhappy and unfulfilled existence, I didn't want that future.

My heart was palpitating so violently that the vibrations were making my chest ache. I couldn't speak, as my throat felt like it had been tied up in all that cabling covering the piano. My hands were shaking vigorously. I fluffed all the notes, and my timing was about as precise as a dad trying to dance at a wedding. But I had *done it* (with the piano turned on this time), and to my amazement, nothing bad had happened as a result.

It is fair to say that Meldrew did not respond well to this. For the first time in my life, he wasn't in control. I was. The more confident I became, the more he fought back. But I had begun to match his strength, and each time I turned the volume up on that piano, another part of him was silenced.

Five years, 183 packets of crisps, and 1788 shameless chocolate biscuits later, all in the form of social bribes, I finally ventured across the street and played the piano in that café. About a week later, the whole world went into lockdown, as the Covid-19 pandemic was in full swing. I like to think that my playing wasn't responsible, but it was hard not to take it personally.

As I sat at home, locked down, marinating in my memories of the outside world, that studio was always in the forefront of my mind. If they were being sensible, then they'd use the opportunity of businesses being closed and everyone staying home to get round to decorating it properly. But as much as that flawed decor bothers my OCD, I suppose it has made me realise that perfection is never the goal in life. That studio (hard as it is for me to believe) is all perfectly practical. The fact that it isn't all practically perfect really doesn't matter. Just like me, nothing needs 'fixing'.

There is nothing inherently bad about me. I just have a few characterful oddities, like a quirky disused cat flap in a door, that makes the me-ness of me so special.

Meldrew will always be there, as nothing will ever be enough for him. But – he challenges me to match my own strength to his. Not only has my confidence grown in my music, but it has grown through every other part of my life as well. The thing that has been remarkable about working with my anxiety is that I have discovered strength I never knew I had. I may not have conquered the music industry, but I have begun to conquer my anxiety.

Not all therapists look like they belong in certificate-clad offices with a long couch and an array of fake plants. Sure, plenty of them do, and there's nothing wrong with that. But some therapists stack shelves in supermarkets. Others work in accountancy. Some therapists have four legs and meow.

It doesn't matter what your therapist looks like, because listening can save just as many lives as talking can.

I would never have believed you, if you had told me that one of the best therapists I'd ever encounter would be a music producer. But it's true, and he continues to save me from myself everyday.

Mad to be Normal

Ad Astra

There were children of the sun
The moon and the earth
You were none of those
But a child that the stars birthed

Charlotte R Faulconbridge

Playlist for Chapter 11

Rocket Man, Elton John

New Horizons, The Moody Blues

Free Bird, Lynyrd Skynyrd

Things Can Only Get Better, D:Ream

The Origin Of Love, Stephen Trask

A long time ago in a galaxy far, far away...[1] a smaller galaxy plunged straight through its heart, sending shockwaves rippling throughout space. Moving at high speeds, the force of these two galaxies colliding swept up gas and dust, creating an exploding starburst around them, like an astronomical firework. These two bright young things crashed into each other and created one gigantic galaxy – a never-before-seen spectacle, now known as the cartwheel galaxy. One of the most complicated galactic systems, the cartwheel galaxy is far from normal.

Complicated doesn't have to be bad. Complicated means compelling, elaborate, and fascinating. And normal, well: what even *is* normal? You'd have to be mad to want to be normal! Surely, normal is an unquantifiable ineffability.

Because of the cartwheel galaxy's spectacular stellar shaping, it is tricky to classify. Like our own Milky Way, it is sometimes seen as a spiral galaxy, whereas in other areas, it looks elliptical. Lenticular galaxies sit somewhere in the middle; they don't fit into a definitive box. Being irregular certainly doesn't detract from the cartwheel galaxy's breath-taking appearance. Some might say that its differences are what makes it so special.

---

1. 489.2 million light years away from Earth, to be exact.

When my autism diagnosis hit me, I thought it was going to be catastrophic; like my life was about to implode, never to be the same again. But my diagnosis isn't what *made* me autistic. I had always been this way – nothing was ever going to change that – and now I could show the world my true self.

My diagnosis helped me understand why I had always felt a bit too alien for Earth, but a bit too human for outer space. I realised that to be accepted, I didn't have to fit inside a particular box. Like the cartwheel galaxy, I could be my own unique phenomenon. A lenticular in a sky full of spirals.

Whilst this revelation was a beautiful one, it was also heart-breaking, because I realised that I didn't know myself at all. My authentic self had always been there, buried beneath all the different masks I had worn throughout the course of my life, but I had to unlearn everything about the person I thought I needed to be, in order to discover where I belonged. Unmasking isn't just about acknowledging the truth of who we are. It is about accepting that truth, and being proud of it. It is about having the confidence within ourselves to live fearlessly, regardless of how we are treated along the way.

No, not everyone is going to like you. Some people will never understand. Some people will never 'get' you. Some people will never appreciate how hard just existing actually is. But continuing to live our lives fearlessly, despite this, is the most powerful thing we can do.

The longest relationship we will ever have is with ourselves – and if we can't make it with *us*, then we won't be able to make it with anyone else. By learning to love exactly who I am, and by showing my authentic self to the world, the universe rewarded me by attracting the right people into my life. People that I wouldn't have ever known, if it wasn't for my unveiling, that I could not and would not even want to begin to fathom living without. The loudest way to love someone is to tell them to be themselves. Go and love someone today!

I was made to do *different* things. Things that I couldn't do if I was neurotypical, because I, myself, was made differently. Being different was never the sin. The sin was being blind to how remarkable that gift was. And yes, I do see my autism – and all autism – as a gift. I don't think many people realise just how freeing it feels to be unapologetically myself. Because I am neurodivergent, I am not confined to the realms of other people's expectations. I can set my own boundaries, where there are no limits.

I don't want you to mistake 'acceptance' as an act in which only the good parts are accounted for. True acceptance is being able to accept the bad days that come with the good. Otherwise, it would be too easy to only love the good bits about ourselves! Sometimes I find it really hard to love my autism. There are days when the positives make up for all my challenges, but there are also days when the positives *definitely* don't outweigh the negatives. But there is never a day when I can't find a positive. Sometimes you only need *one*. Even if the positive entities in your life don't completely erase the negatives, you still have some positives. That should never be underestimated.

Autism has become my ultimate get-out-of-normal-free card; it was never a tragedy. I have one of the most unique opportunities in the world – not to *use* it would be the real tragedy.

If you're reading this and you're feeling ashamed of your weird and wacky existence, then you're not alone. I used to think that I was quite extraordinarily freakish. After all, I was the girl who collected barcodes. The girl who fell in love with a car; who had a favourite ruler. But after spending a considerable amount of time studying humanity's wacky behaviours, I came to the conclusion that everyone is just bloody bonkers. This meant that I was really quite ordinary. Disappointing really.

Somebody I went to school with used to eat paper. Good for them! Finding a snack with absolutely no calories whatsoever is Nobel-Prize-winning material. One of my exes liked to dry themselves after a shower with a hairdryer instead of a towel. Some might say this is ridiculous – but not only is it more effective at drying your skin, it's also more hygienic, because towels left in steamy bathrooms are harbingers of bacteria. The moment he pointed this out to me, in that moment he became instantaneously more attractive. Anyone who points out a new way to be more sanitary automatically gets put into my good books. I know a lady who regularly has her dog lick her feet. Congratulations on making the rest of us look like idiots splurging on expensive reflexology treatments, when you discovered a cheaper alternative long ago.

The point I'm trying to make here is that all these people I'm talking about are 'neurotypical'. *Normal does not exist* – so stop trying to fight yourself, and start fighting for yourself. Even the most typically mundane person on the planet will have a streak of exuberance somewhere; it may just be in deep cover, camouflaged by their company car and corporate-branded biro.

Like the cartwheel galaxy, my label doesn't define me, and I don't let others define me by my diagnosis either. I am defined by my talents, the quirky way I see the world, and sometimes, my obsession with cats. Adversity has become my ally.

When it comes to bliss, I must admit I'm a communist. I am at peace with myself. Yes, there will be many more storms that I'll have to shelter from, but through sunshine and through shadow, I will never *never* hide myself away again.

I was never a broken neurotypical person. I was always a perfect autistic person.

Afterword

Well, this book has been *a process*.

I started writing on my 21st birthday in 2020, and we are now around heading towards the end of 2023. In that time, I have gone from initially planning to publish this book under a pseudonym, wanting to disregard any ownership or resemblance that it held to my life, to wanting to claim every part of it as belonging to me: the good, the bad, and the socially ugly.

To say that I was terrified about letting the outside world into my universe is an understatement. But perhaps not for the reasons expected.

I like 'big talk'. Small talk has just never been my thing. So surprisingly, talking about depression, anxiety, and all that lovely stuff is a lot easier than confessing to the masses my philosophical rationale regarding the imminent development of a third leg. Or that I can remember being born. Or that I actually pretended to be dead in order to avoid briefly talking to a stranger.

Those little things that make the me-ness of me, well, *me*... those are the things not many of us talk about openly, simply because they're our quirky, private, oddities. *But we all have them.*

As I mentioned in the Introduction, writing this book really has been one huge exercise in exposure therapy – due to my newly found confidence, this book has given me the knowledge and power to embrace my identity to the maximum.

Remember the girl who was mute? The one who had to starve herself before every performance, so she could play music in front of people? Well, she is now performing at open-mic events nationally; she's had successful poetry publications; she's hosting an online safe-space where disabled and neurodivergent creatives can share their talents, and embarking on creating resources for autistic people and educational providers to improve their development of inclusive SEND support.

To find out more about my work within changing perceptions surrounding disabilities, visit:

https://www.inclusivecreatives.co.uk/

Acknowledgements

Firstly, to everyone who has ever supported me on my journey – whether you've been there from the very start; if I've only just had the pleasure of meeting you; or if we are yet to meet: *thank you.*

I cannot allow to go unnoticed the incredible team of talent who helped put this book together, so thank you to Is Andrews, Rebecca Murter, and Brit Scott, for putting your hearts and souls into bringing the dust of my imagination into physical reality.

I must then thank Sarah Hodgkinson, the woman without whose poetic influence I would never have pursued my writing, in any shape or form. (I still treasure that Ted Hughes quote you gave me when we first met, and I read it whenever I need reminding of this!)

Thank you to Dr Michael Reddish, for never straying from your principles, and for always sticking up for the truth of what's right.

Debra Quinn, thank you for helping to encourage my creative pursuits when I doubted my abilities, and for showing me that therapy can be more than just talking!

To Mary Tynan, for not just showing me the magic of numbers, but the magic of wisdom.

Thank you to Al Rendle, for sharing your space with me so I didn't have to hide, but so I could shine. *And* for introducing me to the next man on this list...

...who is *not* a medical professional, but who still manages to save lives – thank you, James Cannock, for saving mine.

Stephen Perrins, you made me fall in love with music all over again, a love I thought I'd lost forever. *Thank you for the music.*

Thank you, Clare De Souza, for reuniting me with my voice.

Amanda Goddard, thank you for not trying to fit me into a standardised box. You helped create a box shaped *perfectly* for me.

Kylie Holdback, you have *always* been ringside whenever I needed someone to fight in my corner. So thank you for that, and for also kicking extreme amounts of arse in almost every direction you happen to walk in.

I physically wouldn't have survived the worst years of my chronic illness without Dr Peter Townsend and David Dickins. You were both there for me whenever I needed help, no matter how challenging the situation. Thank you.

Of course I have to thank my cats, Tigger (RIP), Bailey, Tiger-Lily, Apollo and Sputnik, for distracting me during the writing process with your endless need for affection. This book probably would have been finished six months earlier if none of you had intervened. Come to think of it, why am I thanking you?

Mum, I could write an *entire* book dedicated to how thankful I am for you, which in a strange way, is sort of what I have done. If it wasn't for you, then I would never had been brave enough to keep going, so there wouldn't have been a story for me to tell. *You are my author.*

I would also like to thank the rest of my family for continuingly allowing me to be myself, no matter how weird and wonderful that may look.

And finally, and rather begrudgingly, I must thank my inner chimp, Meldrew, for stoking the fire that inspires me to keep burning.

About the Author

Charlotte R Faulconbridge is a prize-winning poet, author and musician. She lives with her two dogs, four cats, and three owls.

As well as being autistic, Charlotte suffers from high-functioning anxiety, dyspraxia, sensory processing disorder, myalgic encephalomyelitis, and a worsening cat addiction... After being disagnosed with a debilitating chronic illness in her early teens, she found peace within writing; processing her trauma and discovering strength and power in her pain has become the lifeblood of her work. Charlotte has already made an impression on the poetry scene as a newcomer, with her quirky and often heartbreakingly raw performances. She advocates for inclusion within the poetry community, often performing her poems in British sign language (BSL) and sign-supported English (SSE).

Too High to Function is Charlotte's first book.